Praxis® 5039 English Language Arts Content and Analysis

How to pass the Praxis® 5039 by using relevant test prep, proven strategies, practice test questions, and constructed response examples.

By: Kathleen Jasper, Ed.D.

Kathleen Jasper LLC
Estero, FL 33928
http://www.kathleenjasper.com | info@KathleenJasper.com

Praxis® 5039 English Language Arts Content and Analysis: How to pass the Praxis® 5039 by using relevant test prep, proven strategies, practice test questions, and constructed response examples.

Printed in the United States of America
ISBN: 9798596844016

Thank you for taking the time to purchase this book. I really appreciate it.

Would you mind leaving a review?

Did you purchase this book on Amazon? If so, I would be thrilled if you would leave an unbiased review at your convenience. Did you purchase this book from KathleenJasper.com? If so, you can leave a review on Facebook, Google, or directly on our website on the product page. Thank you for using my products.

Visit my Facebook Page.

I post videos, practice test questions, upcoming events, and other resources daily on my Facebook Page. Join us every Tuesday at 5 P.M. ET for our Facebook live math help session. https://www.facebook.com/KathleenJasperEdD.

Check out my other products.

I have built several comprehensive, self-paced online courses for many teacher certification exams. I also have other books, webinars and more. Go to https://kathleenjasper.com and use offer code **ENGLISH20** for 20% off any of my products.

Join my private Facebook group.

Are you trying to become a teacher and are you looking for a community? Share insights, strategies and connect with other prospective teachers.

Go to: www.facebook.com/groups/certificationprep/ to request access.

Subscribe to my YouTube channel

Check out my enormous video library with tons of interesting and insightful content for teacher certification exams and more.

Subscribe here https://www.youtube.com/kathleenjasperedd.

If you have any questions, don't hesitate to reach out. It will be my pleasure to help.
Good luck on your exam.

–Kathleen Jasper, Ed.D.

This page intentionally left blank.

Table of Contents

This page intentionally left blank.

How to Use this Book

Often people will purchase a study guide and become overwhelmed with the amount of information and tasks within the guide. Below is a suggested way to use the book.

Step 1: Use the practice test at the end of the guide as a pretest. Do this first to measure your skills. This will be a baseline score.

- Take the practice test.

- Mark the ones you get incorrect, but DO NOT look at the correct answers or explanations. That way you can reuse this test later.

- Record your score. This will be your raw score out of 130 because there are 130 questions on the practice test.

- Determine the subareas and objectives in which you are low.

Step 2: Begin your studies with your strengths and weaknesses in mind.

- Start with Content Category I.

- Read the information under each section. That information is very important.

- Work through all the information in the sections in the guide.

- Complete the 10 practice problems at the end of each content category. If you get less than 80% correct, go back through and review content category.

- Do this for all sections of the book.

Step 3: Once you've worked through the entire guide, take the practice test again.

- Work backwards starting with the answer choices first. Eliminate bad words, focus on good words. Then read the question stem.

    Check your answers and read ALL the answer explanations. There is a ton of information in the answer explanations, so even if you get the answer correct, read the explanation.

- Review information as needed.

Step 4: Focus on the constructed response.

- Work through the constructed response prompts.

- Check your writing against the rubric provided.

QUICK TIPS: These tips are represented with a megaphone and include tips and vocabulary you need to know or strategies for answering questions for a particular skill or content category.

 TEST TIPS: Test tips are represented with a light bulb and are specific test taking strategies that can be, and should be, used while taking the exam.

 THINK ABOUT IT: These tips are not necessarily tested concepts, but they provide background information to help make sense of concepts and give necessary information to help answer questions on the exam.

 CAUTION: Caution tips explain what to avoid when selecting your answer choices on the exam. Test writers are very good at creating distracting answer choices that seem like good options. We teach you what to watch for when it comes to *distractors* so you avoid these pitfalls.

Don't forget to look over the Reference Pages

I have included a Good Words List before practice test one. This is a list of words, terms, and phrases that are typically in correct answer choices on this exam. There is also a Bad Words list, which contains words and phrases to avoid. Use the list to *think like a test maker*, *not a test taker* and to be strategic on the exam.

I have also included a reference sheet that includes eminent authors, major works, and dates. This will help you with questions that are specific to certain authors included in the literary canon.

About the Test

The Praxis® English Language Arts: Content Knowledge (5039) is designed to assess standards-based knowledge of skills and competencies of English teachers. The assessment is comprised of 3 content categories and a constructed response section. The following table provides an overview of the assessment.

Test at a Glance

Test Name	English Language Arts: Content Knowledge
Test Code	5039
Time	2 hours and 30 minutes
Number of Questions	130 selected-response questions 2 Constructed Response (essays)
Format	Single selection, multiple selection, selected response, order/match, audio stimulus, video stimulus, table/grid, and select in passage
Test Delivery	Computer delivered

Content Category	Approx. Number of Questions	Approx. Percentage of Exam

I. Reading
  A. Literature
  B. Informational Text and Rhetoric
	48 SR and 1 CR	40%

II. Language Use and Vocabulary	33 SR	19%
III. Writing, Speaking, and Listening	49 SR and 1 CR	41%

I. Reading

I. Reading – A. Literature

1. Major works and authors of United States, British, World, and young adult literature

2. Historical, cultural, and literary contexts of major works and authors of United States, British, and World literature

3. Characteristics of primary literary genres

4. Characteristics of major literary genres

5. Using textual evidence

6. Themes in a variety of genres

7. Literary elements

8. Figurative language

9. Poetic devices and structure

10. Reading strategies that support comprehension

11. Research-based strategies for reading instruction

12. Literary theories

1. Major works and authors of United States, British, World, and young adult literature

Below is a list of the main literary movements and the most common authors and works from those eras. It is impossible to memorize every author and title for every piece of literature out there. The best approach is to understand the defining characteristics of the major movements and some of the prolific writers of those periods. You will be asked one or more questions about authors, works, and literary movements on the test.

Classicalism (1200 BCE – 455 CE)

Classical works are the original works of philosophers and poets. Classicism refers generally to a high regard for a classical period and classical antiquity. Ancient Greek literature refers to literature written in the Ancient Greek language from the earliest texts until roughly the rise of the Byzantine Empire. This period of Greek literature stretches from Homer until the 4th century B.C. and the rise of Alexander the Great.

Quick Tip

Long after the classical period is over, writers continue to imitate the style of classical authors. This tradition of imitation is where we get the term neoclassical, or new classics.

- **Authors/works:**
    - Homer – *The Odyssey* and *The Iliad*
    - Plato – *The Republic*

*Note: Several Greek classics focus on flowers. One example is the Greek myth of *Hyacinthus and Apollo.*

Romanticism/American Renaissance (1800 – 1850)

Romanticism is characterized by dense symbolism and a supernatural, mysterious, sometimes dark tone. There are several elements to Romanticism (Beck et al., 2010): belief in the individual and common man, love of (reverence for) nature, interest in the bizarre, supernatural and gothic, interest in the past, and optimism about the world.

- **Authors/works:**
  - Edgar Allen Poe, various short stories and poems
  - Herman Melville, *Moby Dick*
  - Nathaniel Hawthorne, *The Scarlett Letter*

Realism (late 1800s – early 1900s)

Realism is characterized by the idea that literature should report what happens in a realistic way without judgment. During this time period, authors began writing works where the stories, or plots, were simple and were secondary to the characters; the characters tended to be from the lower or middle class. There is a heavy use of journalistic techniques such as objectivity and reporting facts.

- **Authors/works:**
  - Mark Twain, *The Adventures of Huckleberry Fin*
  - Stephen Crane, *The Red Badge of Courage*

Naturalism (Late 1800s – Early 1900s)

Born out of Realism, Naturalism was a reaction against Romanticism and Victorian literature. Its major characteristics include an emphasis on social Darwinism and the inescapability of heredity and class. Most of the works produced during this movement are in the form of novels.

- **Authors/Works:**
  - Edith Wharton, *Ethan Frome*
  - Jack London, *Call of the Wild*

Modernism (1900s – 1960s)

Modernism breaks from traditional ideas and celebrates individualism and experimentation. This movement arose in the late 19th and early 20th century and is known for criticizing the writing of the early 19th century. A salient characteristic of modernism is self-consciousness. Stream of consciousness became widespread as a literary technique during the Modernist movement that flourished in the years just before and then after World War I (the early to mid 20th century).

- **Authors/works:**
  - Jack Kerouac, *On the Road*
  - Scott F. Fitzgerald, *The Great Gatsby*
  - Virginia Woolf, *A Room of One's Own*
  - William Faulkner, *A Rose for Emily*

Quick Tip

Often associated with the Modernist era, stream of consciousness writing is a technique where the author writes out the thoughts and emotions of the narrator or character as an inner monologue. An example of a novel that uses stream of consciousness writing is *On the Road* by Jack Kerouac.

Transcendentalism (1830 – 1850)

Unique to America, this movement embraced the idea that constructs of society were standing in the way of a truly free existence. Through imagination and a physical separation from these barriers, the mind could transcend into true enlightenment. Visionaries, intellectuals, scholars, and writers in New England in 1836 would come together regularly to discuss spiritual ideas.

- **Authors/works:**
    - Henry David Thoreau, *Waldon* and *Civil Disobedience*
    - Margaret Fuller, *Woman in the 19th Century*
    - Ralph Waldo Emerson, *Self Reliance*

Harlem Renaissance (1920s – 1930s)

Harlem Renaissance was an African American cultural movement of the 1920s and early 1930s that was centered in the Harlem neighborhood of New York City. This literary movement is important because it was the first time in American cultural tradition that the voice of African Americans was front and center. The art, music, and poetry focused on the jazz scene, but more importantly, the challenges of Black Americans were voiced.

- **Authors/works:**
    - Langston Hughes, various poems and short stories such as "Thank You Ma'am," "Dreams," "Mother to Son," "I, Too"
    - W.E.B. Dubois, *John Brown, The Souls of Black Folks*
    - Zora Neale Hurston, *Their Eyes Were Watching God, Dust Tracks on the Road, How It Feels to Be Colored Me*

Surrealism (1920s – 1940s)

Beginning as an artistic movement in Paris in the 1920s and lasting until the 1940s, artists in this movement attempted to bridge reality and the imagination. Surrealism, like the Harlem Renaissance, was both a visual art and literary movement. Salvador Dali is a well-known artist of this era, and his art is characterized by a dream-like quality that juxtaposes images from reality into something imaginary. Andre Breton, listed below, is considered the founder of the Surrealist movement.

- **Authors/works:**
    - Andre Breton, *First Manifesto of Surrealism*
    - Georges Bataille, *The Tears of Eros*
    - Giorgio de Chirico, The Nostalgia of the Infinite

Structuralism (20th Century)

Structuralism is the methodology that implies elements of human culture must be understood by way of their relationship to a larger, overarching system (Poetry Foundation, 2019). It is a movement of thought in the humanities, widespread in anthropology, linguistics, and literary theory, and influential in the 1950s and 1960s.

- **Authors/works:**
    - Roland Barthes, *Mythologies*
    - Roman Jacobson, *The Framework of Language*

Decades in American literary history each have their own iconic literary works. The list below is certainly not an exhaustive list; however, these are works you should know for the exam.

Quick Tip

Claude Levi-Strauss is widely regarded as the father of structural anthropology. His book, *Structuralism and Ecology,* detailed the tenets of what would become structural anthropology.

- **Roaring 20s**
    - *The Great Gatsby* by F. Scott Fitzgerald—an iconic novel that highlights the decadence and excess of the era—the American dream — and serves as a cautionary tale.
    - *The Wasteland* by T.S. Eliot—a comment on the unraveling of personal and, ultimately, societal values.

- **Depression Era 1930s**

  - *Grapes of Wrath* by John Steinbeck—a realist novel that depicts the bleakness and desperation of American life during the Great Depression.

  - *Their Eyes Were Watching God* by Zora Neale Hurston—an honest look at the life of Black Americans in a Black southern town.

  - *Brave New World* by Aldous Huxley—an iconic dystopian novel that outlines the dangers of loss of individuality due to technology and governmental control.

  - *The Hobbit* by J.R.R Tolkien—a children's fantasy novel in which the main character leaves the safety of home to undertake a heroic quest, resulting in personal growth.

- **1940s**

  - *1984* by George Orwell—a dystopian fantasy novel that paints the future as a disturbing idealistic society devoid of individualism.

  - *Animal Farm* by George Orwell—an allegory centered on the Russian Revolution.

  - *Death of a Salesman* by Arthur Miller—a drama that juxtaposes reality and illusion when pursuing the American Dream.

- **1950s**

  - *Catcher in the Rye* by J.D. Salinger—a novel that has themes of alienation, the challenges of growing up, and the shallow nature of society.

  - *Fahrenheit 451* by Ray Bradbury—a dystopian novel in which knowledge is destroyed and the appearance of happiness is paramount.

  - *Night* by Elie Wiesel—a memoir detailing the horrors of the Holocaust.

  - *Raisin in the Sun (drama)* by Lorraine Hansberry—a play set during the Civil Rights Movement of the 1950s that addresses segregated housing by detailing the struggles of a Black family in a Chicago suburb.

- **1960s**

  - *To Kill a Mockingbird* by Harper Lee—a coming-of-age novel that addresses the prejudice prevalent in society and the judicial system.

  - *A Wrinkle in Time* by Madeline L'Engle—a young adult fantasy-adventure tale that plays with the space-time continuum through the eyes of a 14-year-old girl.

  - *I Know Why the Caged Bird Sings*—a 1969 autobiography describing the early years of American writer and poet, Maya Angelou.

Quick Tip

Raisin in the Sun author, Lorraine Hansberry and *I know Why the Caged Bird Sings* author, Maya Angelou, were influenced by the Harlem Renaissance movement, but these authors came later and are part of the Civil Rights movement of the late 1950s and 1960s.

2. Historical, cultural, and literary contexts of major works and authors of United States, British, and World literature

Many of the historical authors are mentioned in the other sections of this book and are not included in this section. These additional authors and works are commonly used in secondary English language arts classroom instruction. This is by no means an exhaustive list of the American literary canon (major literary works). This list has been created to help you with this exam.

Quick Tip

It is important to incorporate multicultural content in instruction because every student in the classroom should feel represented and included.

American Multiculturalism

Author	Works
Paula Gunn Allen (Poems, feminism)	"America the Beautiful: Last Poems" "Pocahontas: Medicine Woman, Spy, Entrepreneur, Diplomat" "The Woman Who Owned the Shadows"
Isaac Asimov (Russian-born American immigrant who made contributions to the sci-fi genre)	*Star Trek* *I, Robot*
Robert Frost (Poems)	"Fire and Ice" "The Road Not Taken" "Mending Wall"
Nathaniel Hawthorne	*The House of the Seven Gables, A Romance* *The Scarlet Letter, A Romance*
Edgar Allen Poe (Poems and short stories)	"The Raven" "Annabel Lee" "Lenore" "The Black Cat" "The Tell-Tale Heart" "The Cask of Amontillado" "The Fall of the House of Usher" "The Masque of the Red Death"

Author	Works
Thomas Pynchon (short stories and novels)	*V.* *The Crying of Lot 49* *Gravity's Rainbow*
John Steinbeck (Novels and novellas)	*Cannery Row* *Of Mice and Men* *The Grapes of Wrath* *The Pearl*

Latino American

Author	Works
Miguel de Cervantes	*Don Quixote*
Sandra Cisneros	*House on Mango Street*
Gabriel García Márquez	*One Hundred Years of Solitude*

African American

Author/Orator	Works
Maya Angelou (Autobiography, poems)	*I Know Why the Caged Bird Sings*
Gwendolyn Brooks (Poems)	"The Mother" "We Real Cool" "To Be in Love"
Paul Laurence Dunbar (Poems)	"Sympathy" "We Wear the Mask"
Alice Douglas (Poems and short stories)	"Everyday Use"
Frederick Douglass (Autobiographies, speeches)	*Narrative of the Life of Frederick Douglass, an American Slave* "Self-Made Men" – 1859 "What to the Slave is the Fourth of July" – Rochester, NY, July 5, 1852

Author/Orator	Works
Nikki Giovanni (Poems)	"Love Is" "Choices" "You Came, Too" "When I Die" "Knoxville Tennessee"
Dr. Martin Luther King Jr. (Letters, speeches)	"Letter from Birmingham Jail" – June 12, 1963 "I Have a Dream" – Washington, DC, August 28, 1963 "Our God is Marching On" – Selma, AL, March 25, 1965 "Beyond Vietnam: A Time to Break the Silence" – New York, NY, April 4, 1967 "The Other America" – Stanford, CA, April 14, 1976 "I've Been to the Mountain Top" – Memphis, TN April 3, 1968

Asian American

Author	Works
J.W and J.D. Houston	Farewell to Manzanar
Amy Tan	*Joy Luck Club*

British

Author	Works
Jane Austen (Social commentary novels)	*Pride and Prejudice* *Emma* *Sense and Sensibility*
The Brontë Sisters	*Collected Poems of the Bronte Sisters*
Emily Brontë (Novel, poems)	*Wuthering Heights* "All Hushed and Still Within the House"
Charlotte Brontë	"Jane Eyre"
Anne Brontë	"Agnes Grey"
Lewis Carroll	*Alice's Adventures in Wonderland* *Through the Looking-Glass*

Author	Works
Geoffrey Chaucer	*Canterbury Tales*
Charles Dickens	*A Tale of Two Cities* *David Copperfield* *Great Expectations*
E. M. Foster	*A Room with a View* *Howards End* *Passage to India*
C.S. Lewis	*Chronicles of Narnia: The Lion, the Witch, and the Wardrobe*
William Shakespeare (Poems and sonnets)	"Romeo and Juliet" "Macbeth" "Julius Caesar" "Hamlet" "A Midsummer Night's Dream" "Much Ado About Nothing"
Virginia Woolf	*Mrs. Dalloway* *A Room of One's Own*
William Wordsworth (English romantic poet)	*Lyrical Ballads, with a Few Other Poems*

Test Tip

Shakespearean (traditional English) sonnets were written in iambic pentameter. Iambic pentameter refers to a pattern of line of poetry in which the emphasis is placed on certain syllables.

Author	Works
Leo Tolstoy	*War and Peace* *Anna Karenina* *The Death of Ivan Llyich*
Vasily Levshin	*Newest Voyage*
Mikhail Shcherbatov	*Journey to the Land of Ophir*

Test Tip

These Russian authors are known for addressing utopian societies using imagery voyages.

3. Characteristics of primary literary genres

When teaching language arts to middle and high school students, teachers should choose a variety of informational and literary text. Effective language arts teachers guide students in making connections between and among texts of different genres.

What is a genre?

A genre is a category of artistic composition, as in music or literature, characterized by similarities in form, style, or subject matter. The main genres recognized in English language arts instruction are fiction, nonfiction, poetry, and dramas. Subgenres are particular categories within a genre. For example, historical fiction is a subgenre of fiction.

Quick Tip

Remember, English teachers should use a balanced literacy approach, which means they use both literary and informational text in the classroom.

- Literary text = fiction
- Informational text = nonfiction

Terminology

Authors use different structures with the intent to organize and structure different types of writing. In poetry, the words are organized into verses and stanzas. In novels, the information is organized in paragraphs and chapters. It is important to recognize that authors use these structures with intent for effect. The structure of the text is often just as important as the words the author chooses to use. Below are common terms used in different literary genres.

Genre	Attributes
Poetry	**Verse.** A single line of a poem **Stanza.** A grouped set of lines in a poem **Rhyme.** Words that have the same sound **Rhythm.** The beat and pace of a poem **Meter.** The number and pattern of emphasis of syllables in a line of poetry **Feet.** A specific number of syllables in a line of poetry.

Genre	Attributes
Drama/fiction	**Plot.** The storyline
	Point of view. The perspective from which the story is told
	Setting. Where and when the story takes place
	Conflict (internal or external). The problem in the story
	Characters. The individuals in the story
	Theme. The main idea of the story
	Dialog. Discussion between characters
	Monolog. Speech by one character
	Prologue. A preface or introduction
	Epilogue. A speech or section at the end to provide a conclusion
	Paragraph. A section of writing with a common theme
	Chapter. A main division of a book
Non-fiction	**Table of contents.** Outline of the text with page references
	Diagrams and pictures. Visual aids to support the text
	Glossary. Definitions of key terms used in the text
	Index. Page references for key terms used in the text

4. Characteristics of major literary genres

The following table provides a list of defining characteristics of major forms within each primary literary genre.

Genre of Writing	Subgenre
Fiction	**Realistic fiction.** Fictional stories that could be true.
	Historical fiction. Fictional stories set during a real event or time in history. These stories will have historically accurate events and locations.
	Science fiction. Fictional stories that focus on space, the future, aliens, and other galaxies.
	Fantasy. Fictional stories that contain monsters, fairies, magic, or other fantastical elements.
Nonfiction	**Informational text.** Text that informs the reader, such as a social science textbook or informational brochure.
	Biographies. Text that tells the life of another person. The author is not the person in the biography.
	Autobiographies. Text that describes one's own life. The author is the person in the autobiography.
	Persuasive writing. Writing that takes a position where the main goal is to persuade the reader to think or believe something.

Genre of Writing	Subgenre
Poetry	**Limerick.** A humorous verse of three long and two short lines rhyming (aabba). **Sonnet.** A poem of fourteen lines using any of a number of formal rhyme schemes. **Epic.** A long narrative that focuses on the trials and tribulations of a hero or god-like character who represents the cultural values of a race, nation, or religious group. **Ballad.** A narrative poem comprised of quatrains. **Haiku.** A Japanese poem consisting of 3 lines and 17 syllables. **Elegy.** Song or poem written to reflect upon a death. It uses elegiac couplets written in honor of someone deceased. **Villanelle.** A nineteen-line poem with two repeating rhymes and two refrains. **Free verse.** A poem that lacks a consistent rhyme scheme or metrical pattern. **Blank verse.** A poem written in a specific meter, written in iambic pentameter that doesn't rhyme
Folklore	**Fable.** A short story that contains animals that speak and act like humans. There is usually a moral at the end of a fable. **Myth.** A story that showcases gods or goddesses and typically outlines the creation of something. **Legend.** A story that may have once been true but is exaggerated, usually about extraordinary human beings. **Fairy tale.** A story that has both human and magical creatures in it.
Dramas	**Comedy.** Entertainment consisting of jokes and satirical sketches, intended to make an audience laugh. **Tragedy.** A play dealing with tragic events and having an unhappy ending, especially one concerning the downfall of the main character.

5. Using textual evidence

Authors deliberately use language to advance their story, point, or argument. This is often accomplished through the use of different literary devices. Literary devices are not reserved just for fictional works. For example, speech writers will use literary devices for effect. A wide range of literary devices and techniques fall under the umbrella of *figurative language*.

Figurative language

Figurative language refers to a word that does not have a normal, literal meaning. It is the opposite of literal language. Figurative language expressions are commonly used in poetry to bring out emotion and help readers form images. Prose and nonfiction writers also use figurative language to make a point.

Device	Definition	Example
Allusion • Biblical • Literary • Historical	An indirect reference to a well-known person, place, or thing from the past	I had no idea my off-handed statement would open Pandora's box.
Metaphor	A direct comparison of two unlike things	The child is the sunshine of her father's life.
Simile	A comparison of two unlike things using "like," "as," or "than."	The child shines like the sun.
Personification	Giving human characteristics to something non-human	The waves tickled the shore.
Onomatopoeia	A word that imitates a real-life sound	Boom! The thunder shook the house.
Idiom	A common saying that is specific to a language	It's raining cats and dogs out there.
Hyperbole	An exaggeration for effect (its opposite is an understatement)	I must have answered a thousand calls today!
Oxymoron	When two contradictory words are put together	bittersweet; silent scream; deceptively honest
Situational irony	An unexpected turn of events.	A police station got robbed.
Verbal irony	A figure of speech when the speaker says something he or she means as the opposite, sometimes sarcastically. Verbal irony differs from situational irony.	Responding, "That's a terrific plan!" when someone suggests something outrageous, like jumping off a cliff.

6. Themes in a variety of genres

Themes in literature

The theme of a literary work is the general idea or premise of the story. There are several common themes in literature:

- Love
- War and peace
- Coming of age
- Good vs evil

- Death
- Courage and perseverance
- Redemption
- Revenge

Common elements in literature

Identifying common images or elements in literature that convey meaning will help to increase understanding of text. For example, water will often represent forgiveness, baptism, and rebirth. Elements of nature can often convey meaning in life and death. The following table provides common elements in literature and their meaning.

Element	Meaning
serpent	the devil or deception
candle	light in darkness
dove	purity or simplicity
window	freedom
rain	sadness
fire	death or pain
apple	temptation

7. Literary elements

Points of view

The point of view of a piece of literature is the perspective from which a story or passage is told. On the exam, you might be required to determine from what point of view a text is told and then analyze how these differing points of view affect the tone and meaning of the text. There are five basic points of view from which a story can be told. The table that follows outlines each of these points of view.

Point of View	Description
First person	• A narrator in the story recounts his or her own perspective, experience, or impressions. • The pronouns *I*, *we*, *me*, and *us* are used in the text.
Second person	• The narrator tells the story to another character or the audience. • The pronouns *you* and *your* are used in the text.
Third person objective	• The narrator remains a detached observer, telling only the story's action and dialogue. • The pronouns *he*, *she*, *they*, and *them* are used in the text.
Third person limited omniscient	• The narrator tells the story from the viewpoint of one character in the story. • The pronouns *he*, *she*, *they*, and *them* are used in the text.
Third person omniscient	• The narrator has unlimited knowledge and can describe every character's thoughts and interpret their behaviors. • The pronouns *he*, *she*, *they*, and *them* are used in the text.

Tone

The tone of a piece of literature is the way the author conveys feelings or attitudes through their writing. A tone can be happy, sad, angry, peaceful, funny, sincere, or many other characteristics. Authors use word choice to affect the tone, attitude, imagery, and voice of their writing so that they can communicate a feeling they want readers to experience when reading their piece.

A single keyword or phrase can make a difference in the way a person feels or imagines a scenario. In this way, their word choice shapes the meaning and the tone of their work. The example that follows shows how different synonyms for happy can communicate different feelings or bring to mind different images.

Test Tip

Make sure you know the difference between the protagonist and antagonist of a story or poem.

Protagonist – The main character of the story, plot, or poem.

Antagonist – The main foe or enemy of the main character of the story, plot, or poem.

Example	Meaning
I am at peace with his choice.	Implies acceptance of a poor decision
I am content with his choice.	Implies satisfaction with the decision
I am pleased with his choice.	Implies smugness toward the decision
I am over the moon with his choice.	Implies excitement over the decision

8. Figurative language

Literary devices are writing, or narrative, techniques that authors use to convey a message and help the reader with the interpretation and understanding of text.

The following is a list of the common literary and rhetorical devices. This is not an exhaustive list by any means, but these are the most common this exam (Literary Devices Editors, 2013):

Device	Definition	Example
Allegory	This is when ideas are used to symbolize people.	The *Hunger Games* is an allegory for humans' obsession with reality TV.
Alliteration	This is the repetition of a consonant sound at the beginning of a word for effect (e.g., sense and sensibility).	"She sells seashells by the seashore."
Allusion	This is a reference to a famous or well-known event or piece of literature to allow the reader to make a connection. There are three types of illusion: biblical, literary, and historical.	"I had no idea my comment would open Pandora's box."

Device	Definition	Example
Anaphora	This is when words or phrases are repeated at the beginning of a clause or sentence.	Martin Luther King's 1963 "I Have a Dream" speech— "*I have a dream* that one day even the state of Mississippi . . . will be transformed into an oasis of freedom and justice. *I have a dream* that my four little children will one day live in a nation where they will not be judged by the color of their skin but by the content of their character. *I have a dream* today!"
Archetypal elements	This is a character that represents some universal patterns. For example, all villains and heroes have certain characteristics. This rhetorical device is often found in myth genres.	*Garden* symbolizes love and fertility. *Light* symbolizes hope.
Assonance	This is the repetition of vowel sounds to create internal rhyme (e.g., please set the kite right).	"try to light the fire"
Cliché	This is a saying or expression that is overused to the point that it has lost its original meaning.	"only time will tell" "At the end of the day…"
Consonance	This is when sounds produced by consonants within a sentence or phrase are repetitive.	chuckle—fickle—kick
Dialect	A regional variety of language distinguished by features of vocabulary, grammar, and pronunciation from other regional varieties.	*Listen, Sam, if it was nature, nobody wouldn't have tuh look out for babies touchin' stoves, would they? 'Cause dey just naturally wouldn't touch it. But dey sho will.*
Diction	This is the distinctive tone and style of an author.	The author might prefer to use formal language instead of informal language such as slang.
Epigraph	This is a quotation located at the beginning of a literary work that gives the reader an idea of what the work is about.	"Behind every great fortune there is a crime" —from *The Godfather*
Euphemism	This is the use of a nicer word or expression to refer to something unpleasant.	Saying *passed away* instead of *died*
Fable	This is the use of animals or objects to teach a moral lesson.	*The Tortoise and the Hare* is an example of a fable.

Device	Definition	Example
Figurative language	This includes simile, metaphor, personification, idioms, and symbolism.	"She is the sun." "He is as strong as an ox."
Flashback	This unveils to the reader what happened in the past.	A character is getting ready to do something and, in that moment, recalls a memory that is related to the present moment.
Foreshadowing	These are hints or warnings the author gives the reader about the outcome without ruining the suspense.	The following is foreshadowing change: *The same old thinking and the same old results.*
Hypophora	This is when a question is raised and immediately answered by the same person.	From E. B. White's Charlotte's Web: "After all, what's life, anyway? We're born, we live a little while, we die."
Irony	This is used to depict a sharp contrast between how things unfold and how they were expected to unfold.	"A teacher fails a test." This is ironic because we expect teachers to pass a test.
Isocolon	This is when two or more phrases have similar structure, rhythm, and length (e.g., veni, vidi, vici).	"signed, sealed, delivered"
Litotes	This is a form of verbal irony—an understatement.	For example, saying "not too bad" when one means "very good."
Mood	This is often confused with tone; mood is not the author's attitude but how the readers are made to feel as a result.	Readers can feel *amused, energetic, excited, blissful*, etc.
Parable	This teaches a moral or religious lesson.	Well-known examples of parable are "The Good Samaritan" and "The Prodigal Son."
Paradox	This is juxtaposing contradictory concepts that, when put together, reveal some hidden truth or significant value.	"Your enemy's friend is your enemy."
Point of view	This is about who tells the story and how that determines the way the story unfolds and influences the tone.	An objective outsider A first-person account A third-person account
Satire	This is when the author is using humor and making fun of a human flaw not to entertain or amuse the reader but to get the reader to feel contempt for the subject. Satire is beyond sarcasm.	An example would be when political cartoons use humor to attack political issues.

Device	Definition	Example
Symbolism	A symbol has layers of figurative meaning to give the object a greater meaning than its literal meaning.	The *dove* is a symbol of peace.
Synecdoche	This is a term for when a part of something refers to the whole of something or vice versa.	An example would be using the word "suit" to refer to the businesswoman.
Syntax	This is the physical placement of the words and sentences. Grammar is a part of syntax.	Authors can purposefully change the typical subject-verb-object sequence in order to achieve rhythmic, lyrical, or questioning effects.
Tone	This is the perspective or attitude of the author with an intended effect on the reader.	Author's tone can be *joyful, humorous, pessimistic,* etc.

9. Poetic devices and structure

Analyzing poetry

There are several elements to consider when analyzing poetry.

- **Theme.** What is the overall meaning of the poem?
- **Speaker.** Who is the narrator of the poem?
- **Language.** What can be derived from the author's word choice and literary devices?
- **Meter, rhyme, and rhythm.** What is the beat of the poem?
- **Structure.** How are the lines and stanzas organized?
- **Context.** When and where was the poem written? What was happening at that time and place?

When analyzing poetry, it is important to recognize the patterns of the verses and stanzas.

Element	Definition	Example
Stanza	A stanza is a group of lines of poetry.	• Couplet (two-line stanza) • Tercet (three-line stanza) • Quatrain (four-line stanza) • Cinquain (five-line stanza) • Sestet (six-line stanza)
Meter	Meter is the basic rhythm of a line of poetry.	• Spondaic (stressed, stressed) • Trochaic (stressed, unstressed) • Iambic (unstressed, stressed) • Anapestic (unstressed, unstressed, stressed) • Dactylic (stressed, unstressed, unstressed)

Element	Definition	Example
Feet	A foot in poetry is a basic repeated sequence of syllables. The length of feet in a line of poetry is notated in Greek suffixes.	• Monometer (one foot) • Dimeter (two feet) • Trimeter (three feet) • Latetrameter (four feet) • Pentameter (five feet) • Hexameter (six feet) • Heptameter (seven feet) • Octometer (eight feet)

Quick Tip

In poetry, **iambic pentameter** is the most commonly used meter. Famous works in iambic pentameter include:

- Geoffrey Chaucer, *Canterbury Tales*
- William Shakespeare, *Macbeth, Hamlet,* and *A Midsummer's Night Dream*
- John Milton, "Paradise Lost"

Sample critical analysis

In the following section, we examine the poem "Daybreak in Alabama" by Langston Hughes. We provide a critical analysis to evaluate the effect of the literary devices and language elements used in the poem.

Daybreak in Alabama

by Langston Hughes

When I get to be a colored composer
I'm gonna write me some music about
Daybreak in Alabama
And I'm gonna put the purtiest songs in it
Rising out of the ground like a swamp mist
And falling out of heaven like soft dew
I'm gonna put some tall tall trees in it
And the scent of pine needles
And the smell of red clay after rain
And long red necks
And poppy colored faces
And big brown arms
And the field daisy eyes
Of black and white black white black people
And I'm gonna put white hands
And black hands and brown and yellow hands
And red clay earth hands in it
Touching everybody with kind fingers
Touching each other natural as dew
In that dawn of music when I
Get to be a colored composer
And write about daybreak
In Alabama.

Critical analysis of "Daybreak in Alabama"

In nature, living and nonliving things coexist in harmony. Biological diversity is essential for species to survive. Yet, in American society, there is a history of segregation, especially in states like Alabama, where people are separated by race. In the poem, "Daybreak in Alabama," Langston Hughes desegregates Alabama by using imagery and sensory details relating to the environment, the people, and the landscape.

Langston Hughes uses environmental descriptions like, "the scent of pine needles and the smell of red clay after rain," to elicit pleasant feelings about Alabama. He then uses natural references to describe Black people as beautiful, "And long red necks, and poppy colored faces, and big brown arms, and the field daisy eyes." Finally, he integrates races, when he says, "And I'm gonna put white hands, And black hands and brown and yellow hands, And red clay earth hands in it, Touching everybody with kind fingers, Touching each other natural as dew." The term *natural as dew* is another reference to nature, implying that Black and White people living in an integrated society is natural or biological.

While Alabama is often associated with racial segregation, Langston Hughes integrates the southern state in his poem "Daybreak in Alabama." He uses favorable images and smells of Alabama to show Blackness and Whiteness coexisting as natural as the clay after the rain or the dew at daybreak. This poem is a proclamation that integration is like daybreak, a new beginning.

Think about it!

Notice that nowhere in the poem does Langston Hughes say the word *desegregation,* yet the reader derives this meaning from the poem by using a critical approach to analyzing the poem. This requires finding implicit meaning from the literary devices used in the poem.

10. Reading strategies that support comprehension

Learning how to construct meaning is a significant step of the reading process. Students can use a variety of strategies to improve understanding while reading. To become strategic readers, students need to be explicitly taught how to use metacognition.

Strategy	Description
Activating prior knowledge	This pre-reading strategy asks students what they already know about a topic to provide a framework or schema to tie the new information to. A KWL chart—What do you know (K), what do you want to know (W), what did you learn (L)— is helpful for this strategy.
Schema building	Schema is stored clusters of concepts or knowledge from previous experiences. Schema and background knowledge are synonymous. Schema building can be applied in the classroom to improve the learning experience. One way to build schema is to help readers actively relate their own knowledge to ideas in the text.
Clarifying	Also called the "fix-up" strategy, this is a during-reading strategy where students monitor their comprehension by asking questions, rereading, and searching for context clues when the text is confusing.
Generating questions	Students ask and answer questions at key points in the text in this during-reading strategy. This strategy is also effective for facilitating discussion about the text.

Strategy	Description
Paraphrasing	This can happen at key points during reading or after reading. It is similar to retelling and summarizing but takes those strategies a step further by incorporating the new knowledge into student thinking. It is perfect for monitoring comprehension because the student cannot reword what the author said if he or she does not understand what the author said. It is an easy formative assessment to guide future instructional supports.
Analyzing	Analysis happens during close reads and after the reading is over. Students reread key pieces of text with a specific task or question in mind, developing deeper levels of understanding.
Summarizing	This after-reading strategy requires the student to synthesize the details and information presented in the text into a statement that sums up the main idea.

Graphic organizers

A graphic organizer is a visual and graphic display that depicts the relationships between facts, terms, and ideas within a text. Most English teachers use graphic organizers to help students organize information as they read. Graphic organizers are effective for all students, but they are especially effective for visual learners. Common types of graphic organizers include:

KWL charts are used to activate or build background knowledge. KWL stands for:

- **(K)** What do you know?
- **(W)** What do you want to know?
- **(L)** What did you learn?

K Before reading	W Before and during reading	L After reading

Venn diagrams are used to compare and contrast characters, content, or events in the text.

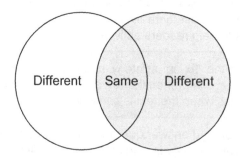

Mind maps are diagrams to visually organize ideas and concepts. The central idea or concept is placed in the center of the diagram, and then related ideas are added.

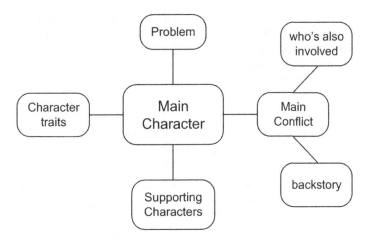

Student response to text

Middle and high school students are in the formal operational stage of development and are reading and analyzing complex literary and informational text. As they derive meaning from text, they also relate the text to their lives, discuss the text with their peers, and write about the text in their journals. The following are several strategies students use to respond to text. You will see one or more of these on the exam.

Activity	Definition	Example
Jigsaw	A cooperative learning activity in which each student becomes an expert on a small piece of information that is part of a much larger piece.	Teachers arrange students in groups. Each group member is assigned a different piece of information. Group members then join with members of other groups assigned the same piece of information and research and share ideas about the information. Eventually, students return to their original groups to try to "piece together" a clear picture of the topic at hand.
Think-pair-share	A cooperative learning activity in which students work together to solve a problem or answer a question about an assigned reading.	**Think** – Teachers begin by asking a specific question about the text. Students "think" about what they know or have learned about the topic. **Pair** – Each student should be paired with another student or a small group. **Share** – Students share their thinking with their partner. Teachers expand the "share" into a whole-class discussion.
Chunking	A reading activity that involves breaking down a difficult text into manageable pieces and having students rewrite these "chunks" in their own words.	A science teacher is working with students on complex science text. Students are overwhelmed by the enormity of the chapter. She has students use a graphic organizer where they write down important phrases and words from each paragraph. Students can then consult the graphic organizer as they move through the text.

Activity	Definition	Example
Reading response journals	A writing activity where students use journals to react to what they read by expressing how they feel and asking questions about the text.	After reading a storybook in class, the teacher asks students to use their reading response journals to respond to the story emotionally, make associations between ideas in the text and their own ideas, and record questions they may have about the story.
Evidence-based discussion	The teacher sets the expectation that students use evidence in the text to support claims they make during the discussion.	The class is discussing World War II. Students are split into groups and answer questions on the board. Students must identify where their answers or claims are supported in the text.
Literature circles	A small-group, cooperative learning activity where students engage and discuss a piece of literature/text.	The teacher divides the class into groups. Every student has a role. The teacher distributes an article from the newspaper. Students read the article and then discuss the article. Students engage using their role to understand the text.

11. Research-based strategies for reading instruction

When developing a balanced literacy approach in the classroom, teachers must use several data points to measure text complexity. It is important that teachers select appropriate text levels because classrooms consist of students with varying abilities.

Determining text complexity

With the adoption of Common Core State Standards, text complexity has become a focus to prepare students for the challenges of reading for college and career. According to Achieve the Core (n.d.), educators should use three steps when choosing text:

1. **Quantitative measures** or data expressed in numbers.
   - Sentence length
   - Readability measures (Flesch Kincaid)

2. **Qualitative measures** or data that is non-numerical in nature.
   - Observations
   - Surveys
   - Standards
   - Anecdotal notes

3. **Professional judgment** or applying relevant training, knowledge, and experience to choosing text and resources for students.

Think about it!

Text complexity does not always mean choosing a high-level, difficult text. Some texts that are relatively easy to read, such as *House on Mango Street* by Sandra Cisneros, have layers of meaning that are complex. Matching text to task is a key component of complexity.

Text leveling systems allow teachers to implement reading strategies to meet students' individual needs. Reading data, both quantitative and qualitative, should be used to make instructional decisions.

Determining text readability

Text readability is a measure to determine how easy or difficult a passage is. Teachers use text readability to decide what texts to choose for instruction. Text readability is composed of 3 distinct components: qualitative measures, quantitative measures, and reader and task (Lapp, Moss, Grant, & Johnson, 2015).

Text Readability	Description	Examples
Qualitative measures	An informed judgment on the difficulty of the text by considering a range of factors, such as the author's purpose, the levels of meaning, structure of the text, language conventions, language clarity, knowledge demands, and the complexity and importance of visual devices.	Student interest surveys, observations, reading response journals
Quantitative measures	Statistical measurements of text such as readability measures, Lexile levels, words per page, Flesch Kincaid.	Reading levels, Lexile levels, number of words per page
Reader and task	A consideration of students' abilities and expectations of the task the students will perform using the text.	Students' mental processing, reading skills, readiness, prior knowledge, and maturity/sensitivity

Metacognition and comprehension

Analysis is a high-level skill that involves several processes in the brain. Teaching students to analyze text is a complex process involving comprehension and metacognition. At times, students struggle to read for surface comprehension, so when they are asked to analyze text, they struggle to know what that means and how to do it. There is no simple checklist to give students for analytical reading. Teachers must model the skills.

Analysis of text involves two crucial processes: metacognition and comprehension.

Metacognition is thinking about thinking or being aware of the thought process. When students have metacognition, they understand the processes in their minds and can employ a variety of techniques to understand text. The most effective way to model metacognition in English language arts is through a read aloud/think aloud strategy. Below are two examples of a read aloud/think aloud strategy. In both scenarios, the teacher is sharing the thought process aloud as she reads.

- A teacher is reading aloud an excerpt from *A Brave New World* by Aldous Huxley. When she gets to complex vocabulary, she stops and shares her thought process, "That's a word I've never seen before. Let me read around it to see if I can figure it out."

- A teacher is reading *Macbeth* by William Shakespeare. When she discovers a connection to the real world, she stops and talks about it. She models the connection between text and the real world.

Comprehension is a high-level cognitive skill essential in analyzing text. Students must make connections, access and apply prior knowledge, and think deeply about the text. This type of critical thinking while reading involves moving beyond memorization; it involves evaluating all elements of the text and deriving meaning from them. Reading comprehension skills include questioning, summarizing, and predicting.

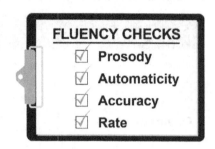

FLUENCY CHECKS

☑ **Prosody**

☑ **Automaticity**

☑ **Accuracy**

☑ **Rate**

- **Questioning.** Having students ask questions based on what they are reading.

- **Summarizing.** Asking students to summarize what they just read in their own words.

- **Predicting.** Asking students what they think will happen next.

*All of the above strategies are considered higher-order/critical-thinking and can be employed before, during, and after reading.

Quick Tip

Modeling is an effective practice for helping students comprehend complex text. When teachers model how to approach difficult text and demonstrate their thought process to students (also known as a read aloud/think aloud), students can then employ those practices during independent reading.

Strategies to promote fluency

Fluency is defined as the ability to read with speed, accuracy, and proper expression, and it is a necessary skill for reading comprehension. For students to understand text, they must first read through the text with fluency. This way, they can focus on meaning rather than sounding out words.

Comprehension is the essence of reading. This is when students begin to form images in their minds as they read. They are able to predict what might happen next in a story because they understand what is happening in the story. Students who are in the comprehension stage of reading do not need to decode (sound out) words. They read **fluently** with **prosody**, **automaticity**, and **accuracy**.

Teachers perform **fluency checks** or **fluency reads** to measure students' reading progress. While the student reads, the teacher follows along. As the student reads, the teacher checks for **automaticity**, which is effortless, speedy word recognition. The teacher also checks the student's **accuracy** and **rate**.

- **Prosody** comprises timing, phrasing, emphasis, and intonation that readers use to help convey aspects of meaning and to make their speech lively. Prosody includes stopping at periods, pausing at commas, reading with inflection, and reading with expression.

- **Automaticity** is the fast, effortless word recognition that comes with repeated reading practice. When students are reading at > 95% accuracy, they have automaticity.

- **Accuracy** is the amount of words a student reads correctly. Typically, accuracy is measured by having students read aloud during a fluency read (also called a running record). The student reads, and the teacher marks any words the student miscues.

- **Rate** is the speed at which students read words correctly. Rate is typically expressed in correct words per minute (wpm).

Fluency and cognitive endurance

Fluency supports cognitive endurance. When students have the cognitive endurance to read through large sections of text and build meaning from that text, they are not wasting cognitive energy on decoding words. Instead, students are reading fluently, using their cognitive energy towards comprehension and critical thinking.

When readers have cognitive endurance, they use less cognitive energy in reading the text and more cognitive energy in developing comprehension. That is why building automaticity and cognitive endurance is essential in developing comprehension.

Effective reading strategies for fluency

- **Readers' theater.** Students read different character's parts in the text.

    - It works best with short stories and dramas (they are already broken into lines for you).

    - Some things to consider when choosing the text for readers' theater:

        o Student interest

        o Readability

        o Matching text to task

Note: If the text is loaded with difficult words, dialect, or antiquated language, the students will not be able to demonstrate accuracy and prosody. Therefore, for readers theater, choose text that students should be able to read at 90-95% accuracy.

Test Tip

Think about readers' theater as a fluency strategy that engages all students. On the exam, you might see readers' theater paired with a drama like *McBeth*, but readers' theater can be used with any text. Each student reads as a different character in the text.

- **Choral reading.** This is reading aloud in unison with a whole class or a group of students. Choral reading is another technique that is low-risk for students and helps build students' fluency, self-confidence, and motivation. As the teacher, you will lead the reading with all students reading in unison. This way, if a student is stumped by a word, they hear you say it correctly, and no one will notice that they cannot. In addition, you can hear if a large group of students is struggling with certain words. This is useful information for future instruction and support.

Ineffective strategies for fluency — Just **say no** to the following strategies on this test.

- **Popcorn reading.** This is randomly calling on students to read whether or not their hands are raised. This could be embarrassing for struggling readers. This can be particularly anxiety-inducing for ELLs.

- **Round-robin reading.** This is when each student takes a turn reading out loud a small portion of the text while the rest of the class reads silently. Research shows this is not an effective activity to increase fluency.

- **Silent sustained reading.** While this can be an effective activity for those who have mastered the text, it is ineffective with a piece of text the student is struggling with.

Test Tip

Remember your bad words and practices. Popcorn and round robin reading are ineffective read aloud practices that may cause students to become anxious, so avoid these on the exam and in your classroom. Typically, you will see questions on the exam that pair silent sustained reading with a struggling student scenario. In that case, it would be the incorrect answer because if students are struggling, silent sustained reading is not the best approach.

English language learners and fluency

Fluency instruction can be beneficial to English language learners (ELLs) because it can simultaneously help enhance their language development. Additionally, ELLs can develop their vocabulary repertoire while practicing reading fluency. Furthermore, while other students read, ELLs can listen and improve their listening comprehension. There are several elements of fluency instruction for language learners and several teaching strategies that can be implemented (Linan-Thompson & Vaughn, 2007). In order to help their learners, teachers should do the following:

- Provide an explicit model of fluent reading.

- Include repeated readings of the same text.

- Provide performance criteria (i.e., speed).

- Choose texts that are not too difficult for ELLs.

Example question

Which strategy is the BEST for supporting fluency in ELL students?

    A. Silent, independent reading

    B. Choral reading of the same text

    C. Round robin reading

    D. Popcorn reading

Correct Answer: B

The best answer here is B. Choral reading of the same text is a way to model fluent reading. The teacher can have students follow along as he/she reads. Choice A is not appropriate because fluency practice is always out loud. Answer choice C is not effective because students who are not fluent will not read the text fluently when it is their turn. It is ineffective and can lead to embarrassment and anxiety. Finally, answer D is incorrect because this exercise puts students on the spot. Popcorn reading can be traumatic for struggling readers.

Instructional approaches and strategies

- **Genre study.** In this approach, the class will conduct in-depth readings of a variety of texts from the same genre in order to understand the characteristics. After a series of genre studies, students should be able to apply their thinking to any of the genres and analyze different genres together to find similar themes or messages.

- **Thematic unit.** A thematic unit will carry a particular theme across a variety of texts and genres.

- **Novel study.** This in-depth study of one particular piece of literature (novel, memoir, autobiography, biography) uses guided and independent reading activities to teach a variety of skills and standards.

- **Interdisciplinary instruction.** Instructional methods that take topics from different content areas and merge them during instruction. Interdisciplinary methods can increase student engagement, critical thinking, and problem-solving skills. Students can also collaborate and work on a project related to this topic. Collaboration should always be encouraged in the classroom, and it is the key to students' success as it promotes learning.

- **Gradual release (I do, we do, you do).** This is when teachers start the lesson by modeling (I do). Then, students work in cooperative groups (we do). Then, students work on their own (you do). The gradual release model is effective because the teacher shows the students what it looks like when the skill is mastered, offers support in guided practice, and gives the students adequate time to practice independently.

- **Directed reading/thinking**. After explaining the activity and modeling it for students, the teacher leads the students into activating prior knowledge by asking questions to help them connect to what they know. This provides schema, or a framework, for new learning. The students make predictions (individually, small-group, or with partners) before reading. After reading the text, they evaluate their predictions to see if they were verified or contradicted. They also find evidence to support that evaluation. This works best with short texts or small chunks of a large text.

- **Question-answer relationships (QAR)**. Students use questions to guide their reading and understanding of text. QAR is broken down into four levels:

    - **Right there.** Questions at this level are the easiest to answer; they are found in the text.

    - **Think and search.** Questions at this level require students to make an inference; this level is a step up from "right there" questions in difficulty.

    - **You and the author.** Questions at this level combine student background knowledge with textual information and are more difficult than think and search questions.

    - **On your own.** Questions at this level are the most challenging because the students must make a judgment statement.

- **Response journals**. Students explore their own thoughts, ideas, and questions about a text through writing. Then, the teacher responds to the students individually through writing in the journal. This is an effective way to give each student specific feedback and get into their heads to see what they are thinking.

- **Semantic mapping.** Students organize their knowledge and experiences around a big idea or topic. The big idea goes in a center circle, and the class brainstorms related subtopics to place in circles surrounding the big idea.

- **Interactive word walls.** Words and definitions are posted on the wall. Students have the opportunity to select words from the wall for different reasons. This helps students interact with their vocabulary.

- **Word sorts.** This is when words are sorted into different categories according to word meaning, sound, or pattern.

- **Cloze.** This is an activity in which words are omitted from the passage, and students are required to fill in the blank. This activity uses semantic and syntactic clues to aid students in completing sentences.

- **Selective highlighting.** This is an effective strategy that can be used to identify important information in text as they read. For example, students can highlight the main idea of the text in one color and the important details of the text in another color.

Quick Tip

An inference is a conclusion that is drawn based on evidence or reasoning – it is an educated guess. Inferences are common in expository texts.

Analyzing student performance on the reading continuum

Reading levels can be used to determine the readability of text, and they are determined by calculating reading accuracy. According to Gunning (2002), these levels include:

- **Frustration level (< 90% word accuracy).** When the text is at the students' frustration level, it is often difficult to comprehend. Students require scaffolding and support, including but not limited to alternate versions of the text, guided graphic organizers, and small group instruction.

- **Instructional level (90% word accuracy).** When the text is at the students' instructional level, the text is challenging to students; however, the students are not frustrated by the difficulty of the text. They are stretching to understand but find the task manageable.

- **Independent level (> 95% word accuracy).** When the text is at the students' independent level, the text is easy to read, and students do not have to stretch or challenge themselves to make sense of the text.

Note: The only way to accurately assess where students fall on the reading continuum is to hear them read aloud individually as you monitor their reading. This is called a fluency check or a running record.

Quick Tip

Cognitive endurance is the use of mental activities and skills to perform tasks such as learning, reasoning, understanding, and remembering. Building cognitive endurance allows readers to use stored cognitive energy for tasks like comprehension. Building cognitive endurance helps students get to the independent reading level or > 95% accuracy.

Teaching fiction

Teaching these story elements helps students understand the text: characters, setting, conflict, rising action, falling action, resolution, point of view, and theme.

- Story maps and plot diagrams are helpful and allow the student to keep track of what is going on, especially in complicated plots. Just be aware that not all fiction falls neatly onto the typical plot diagram.

- Literary elements and genres are also useful for teaching fiction.

Teaching non-fiction and informational texts

- Non-fiction does not have to be read from beginning to end. It lends itself well to the **jigsaw strategy** and close, repeated readings.

- Teaching students text structures (i.e., cause/effect, problem/solution) and how to identify these structures is helpful for student comprehension.

- Teach text features. Illustrations/ photographs with captions, table of contents, maps, graphs, charts, headings, glossaries, and indexes can help students understand the reading, but each aspect has a very specific purpose.

- Strategies such as prediction, clarifying, summarizing, etc., are all useful for teaching students how to break down non-fiction text.

Quick Tip

Literature circles are small, student-led discussion groups about a selected piece of text. Most commonly used for analysis and discussion of complex text, literature circles can also be used for shorter pieces of literature and informational texts. Literature circles also serve as an **assessment tool** as the teacher observes and evaluates collaboration, speaking, participation, reading analysis skills, and outcomes.

When assessing students' understanding of fiction, nonfiction, and informational texts, think beyond multiple-choice tests. While multiple-choice tests are sometimes appropriate, there are other ways to determine if students understand what they read, especially when assessing those higher order thinking skills.

- **Informal/formative**
  - Observations of small group or partner discussions about the text
  - Anecdotal notes based on class discussions
  - Completion of a graphic organizer (KWL, Venn, cause/effect chain, teacher-generated, etc.)
  - Exit tickets/short responses
  - Response journals
- **Summative**
  - Essay response
  - Oral presentation
  - Performance-based assessment
  - Project-based assessment
  - Criterion-referenced

Test Tip

Performance-based assessments are effective for assessing students' understanding of text because it allows students to show mastery while performing a task. For example, students can analyze a play or literary work, write an alternative ending to the story, and then act out the new ending. This boosts creative and critical thinking.

Example question

After a month-long unit on the novel *The Catcher in the Rye* by J.D Salinger, the teacher wants to measure students' mastery of the standards covered while using the novel. Which of the following assessments would be the best to measure these outcomes?

A. A criterion-referenced summative assessment

B. A formative pre-assessment

C. A norm-referenced screening assessment

D. A diagnostic performance-based assessment

Correct Answer: A

The teacher measures standards mastery (criterion-referenced) and outcomes after students read and analyze the novel (summative).

Using technology to teach literacy

The goal of technology integration is always to have the students become proficient. They will need experience and assistance with this. Some strategies for using technology include the following:

- Databases for research sources
- Collaborative activities using shared documents
- Virtual field trips to build background knowledge and schema
- Class blogs to communicate personal experiences
- Digital publishing tools for yearbooks and school newspapers

Technology can be effective in teaching students how to use literary skills digitally and to teach digital literacy. Below are some examples of technology that teachers can implement in their classrooms.

Technology	Description
Blogs	Not only can students publish and share their own writing via a blog, but they can also comment on classmates' writing and get peer and teacher feedback on their writing. This is an authentic, real-world way to bring literacy to life.
Digital books	One way to increase engagement is to ask students to create their own digital books using platforms such as Inkle.
Videos	The teacher can ask students to create a short 30-second video explaining the plot, for example, using music and images. Another way to use videos in class is to have students first read a book and then watch the movie version of the book. Following the movie, the teacher can ask the class to compare and contrast different scenes or characters from the book and the movie.
Digital notetaking	Students can create story maps, plot maps, and mind maps using technology such as shared documents.

12. Literary theories

When readers use a critical approach to literature, they analyze the work with a particular perspective and find meaning that is not explicitly stated. This is essential in building critical thinking and expanding students' perspectives. Often, students can examine a text using multiple approaches. Teachers should encourage and help develop students' skills in using a critical approach when reading.

Critical Approaches to Literature

Approach	Definition
Biographical	This approach relies on understanding the author's life and perspective.
Formalist	This approach examines how the textual elements sync to have the author's intended effect on the reader. Everything needed to analyze and understand the text is located within the text.

Approach	Definition
Gender	This approach delves into the attitudes prevalent in a male-dominated society. When students are reading through this lens, they are looking for evidence of gender inequality and bias.
Sociological	This approach looks at the cultural influences at the time the piece was written. By examining the norms of the culture, the students gain a better understanding of the literature and of the society itself.
Feminist	This approach evaluates the social context and influences on literature through the lens of the female experience.
Historical	Similar to the sociological approach, the historical approach looks at key events of the time and how they influenced the literature. However, this approach also aims to understand how the literary work also affected the people of the time. Did it incite change? Was it shocking?
Psychological	This approach pays special attention to the symbolic meanings that hint at the psyche of the characters and how that drives their motivations throughout the text. Many of Shakespeare's plays lend themselves to a psychological analysis.
Reader-response	This approach takes the perspective that literature is a live thing that relies on and changes with what the reader brings to the interpretation. In this approach, individuals can come up with different interpretations if they read the same texts at different points/ages in their lives. In other words, there is not one right way to interpret text. However, any interpretation must be supported with textual evidence.
Anthropological	This approach focuses on everyday life in various cultures. For example, the focus could be on celebrations or rituals.
Mythological	This approach explores individual imagination using myths and symbols to uncover universal themes. It is strongly connected to social anthropology.

Quick Tip

Effective English teachers encourage students to take a critical approach to literature. Here's an example:

Students are reading a poem containing many water images throughout the text. The poem also describes a woman coming to terms with her childhood. By taking a critical approach, students may infer that the water represents a baptism, or rebirth after the woman accepts her past and moves forward in life. While baptism and rebirth are not mentioned in the text, a critical approach allows students to extract meaning from the poem and use the images of water to support that interpretation.

This page intentionally left blank.

Example Questions and Answer Explanations

1. Homer's Odyssey was published during which literary movement?

   A. Classicalism

   B. Realism

   C. Naturalism

   D. Modernism

2. Langston Hughes, W.E.B. Dubois, and Zora Neale Hurston are all authors associated with:

   A. Structuralism

   B. Modernism

   C. Feminism

   D. Harlem Renaissance

3. This author is most famous for his works *The Raven, Lenore, The Tell-Tale Heart*, and other dark, ghoulish poems and short stories.

   A. Nathaniel Hawthorn

   B. Edgar Allen Poe

   C. John Steinbeck

   D. Robert Frost

4. This is a literary movement that began in Paris in the 1920s when artists attempted to bridge reality and the imagination.

   A. Realism

   B. Modernism

   C. Surrealism

   D. Transcendentalism

5. This book is set in the 1920s on Long Island and examines a version of the American dream that is ultimately unattainable.

   A. *Catcher in the Rye*

   B. *Grapes of Wrath*

   C. *Heart of Darkness*

   D. *The Great Gatsby*

6. The following is an example of:

(Library of Congress)

A. Satire

B. Alliteration

C. Allusion

D. Syntax

7. This is the perspective or attitude of the author with an intended effect on the reader.

A. Tone

B. Setting

C. Sequence

D. Irony

8. Ms. Jackson is working on selecting texts for her students. Her students have varying reading levels. Which of the following is an example of quantitative text complexity measures?

A. Observations of student reading

B. Students' journal entries

C. Students' reading levels

D. Professional judgment

9. Mr. Jensen wants to help students identify important information in the text while they are reading. He wants them to pull out crucial insights to be reviewed after the reading is over. Which of the following would be the most effective strategy for this?

A. Word sort

B. KWL chart

C. Selective highlighting

D. Mind mapping

10. Which of the following would be the most effective way to use the movie The Crucible to support 9th graders who are reading *The Crucible* by Arthur Miller?

    A. Show short clips of the movie to showcase important and complex concepts in the book.

    B. Show the movie in its entirety, and then read the book.

    C. Have students choose between watching the movie or reading the book.

    D. Have students watch the movie at home and read the book in class.

Number	Answer	Explanation
1.	A	Homer's Odyssey is ancient Greek literature and was written in the 4th century, which puts it in the Classical timeframe. Put simply, Homer's Odyssey is very old, which is a characteristic of the Classical time period.
2.	D	Harlem Renaissance was an African American cultural movement of the 1920s and early 1930s that was centered in the Harlem neighborhood of New York City. All three of the authors mentioned are African American artists who wrote during the Harlem Renaissance.
3.	B	Edgar Allan Poe was an American writer best known for his poetry and short stories of mystery and the macabre.
4.	C	Surrealism was a literary movement where artists bridged the real with the imaginary. One artist who is associated with surrealism is Salvador Dali. He juxtaposes real images with fantasy.
5.	D	The Great Gatsby, written by F. Scott Fitzgerald, follows a cast of characters living in the fictional towns of West Egg and East Egg on prosperous Long Island in the summer of 1922. While the characters try to convey wealth and prestige, they are haunted by tragedy. It is described as a cautionary tale of the consequences of the Roaring 20s.
6.	A	Political cartoons fall under the category of satire because they parody serious events and are opinion pieces.
7.	A	The tone is the attitude of the author. Text can have a lighthearted tone, cautionary tone, or cynical tone. The tone depends on how the author writes the story or piece.
8.	C	Quantitative measures are those which represent numbers. Answer choice C is the only quantitative measure listed. All the others are qualitative measures.
9.	C	This is an effective strategy that can be used to identify important information in text as they read. For example, students can highlight the main idea of the text in one color and the important details of the text in another color.
10.	A	Answer choice A is the most effective way to use media to support the students as they read the book. All of the other answer choices use too much of the movie, which can impede students' critical thinking skills while reading the book.

I. Reading – B. Informational Text and Rhetoric

1. How textual evidence supports interpretations of an informational text

2. How organizational patterns and text structures contribute to the central idea in informational texts

3. Word choice and its effect on informational text

4. Rhetorical devices

5. Audience and purpose

6. Written arguments

7. Media and digital literacy

1. How textual evidence supports interpretations of an informational text

Anticipation guides are used as pre-reading, during-reading, and post-reading activities to assess students' knowledge of a subject. Students look at statements from the text and then decide if they agree or disagree. Then they read. When they find the statement or information in the text, they note the page number. After reading, they reflect on whether they agree or disagree.

Statement	Agree or disagree	Page found	Reflection
The Civil Rights Movement was only concerned about voting rights for Black people.	Agree – voting rights were the focus of the movement.	144	I learned that the Civil Rights Movement was concerned with voting rights, discriminating housing policies, unjust employment practices, and more.
Maya Angelou was a prominent Civil Rights Activist	Disagree – Maya Angelou was a writer.	268	I learned that along with her writing, she helped Malcolm X and Dr. Martin Luther King organize marches and events.

Determining meaning based on context

As students encounter complex text, they must use context clues to figure out and understand the text. While students could use a dictionary or glossary to verify their understanding, using these resources each time a student comes across an unfamiliar word is ineffective. Showing students how to access context clues to quickly figure out text is essential in increasing students' comprehension skills. The following are the types of context clues students can use while reading.

Context Clue	Explanation	Example
Restatement	A restatement can be a summary or a paraphrase that can help determine the meaning of unknown words. Context is integral. Keywords such as *in other words* and *that is* signal a restatement.	*He was <u>authoritative</u> with his children—always commanding them to obey him.* In the sentence above, the context following the word *authoritative* provides the restated meaning of the word.

Context Clue	Explanation	Example
Definition	Often, the definition of a word is explicitly stated in the text. However, other times, the reader needs to infer the meaning based on context. Reading a sentence before and after an unknown word can help determine the meaning.	*Plants "eat" by <u>photosynthesis</u>, the process by which plants use sunlight to produce food.* The word *photosynthesis* is defined in this sentence—*the process by which plants use sunlight to produce food.*
Synonym/ antonym	Using synonyms and antonyms is an effective way to determine the meanings of unknown words. If an antonym is given, the reader will see keywords such as *rather than* or *in contrast*. When a synonym is provided, the author might use a semicolon to show the relationship between two similar meanings. Always look at the word in context to help you determine its meaning.	*The <u>fastidious</u> or fussy professor would not accept assignments without the proper heading. (synonym)* *He is very <u>capricious</u>; he always changes his mind about things. (synonym)* *The twins are complete opposites: one is <u>gregarious</u>, and the other is shy. (antonym)* In this case, we can figure out that *gregarious*, the opposite of shy, means outgoing.
Example	Examples of the vocabulary word are often provided in text.	*Meat is an important part of the diet of tigers, wolves, and lions, all of which are <u>carnivores</u>.* In this case, we can infer that carnivores eat meat because there are several examples of meat eaters in the text.

2. How organizational patterns and text structures contribute to the central idea in informational texts

Central idea

The central idea of an informational text is the general topic of the text. The central idea is the text's main focus. **The central idea is not specific. It is a general or broad topic covered in the entire text.** All of the details should support the central idea. In informational text, there is often a thesis statement in the introduction that provides the main idea of the text. It is usually the last sentence of the introduction paragraph.

Key ideas and details

The text's key ideas and details are the pieces of supporting evidence that substantiate the central idea. Key ideas should be tangible examples that explain or support the thesis statement. **Key ideas and details are not general. They are specific pieces of information that support the central idea.**

Text structure and comprehension

Text structure refers to how the information is organized in the text. Understanding text structure and text features can help students with their comprehension. Effective English teachers implement strategies for text analysis in their English curriculum and instruction. If students can identify the clues that tell them the structure of the passage, they can make more sense of the information presented (Dymock, 2005). The following are the main types of text structures.

Text Structure	Description	Clue Words/Phrases
Cause/effect	Authors use this structure to establish a causal relationship between an event and the events that come after.	because of, as a result of, due to, for this reason, in order to, since, the cause, as a result, therefore, then/so, this led to, thus, so, consequently
Chronological/ sequential	Events in this structure are organized chronologically (and sometimes reverse chronological order).	after, at, before, during, finally, first, second, third, last, next, then, until
Compare/ contrast	Authors communicate the similarities and differences among events, concepts, ideas, or people.	more/less, in contrast to, despite, instead of, nevertheless, on the other hand, rather than, similarly, still, though, unlike, as, as opposed to, however, despite, likewise, either/or
Descriptive	Authors use descriptive language to paint a picture for the reader.	for example, for instance, looks like, sounds like, feels like, any descriptive adjectives
Problem/ solution	Authors present an issue or set of issues and possible solutions, then examine the effects of the solutions offered.	because, one part of, as a result, consequently, if/then, remedy, solution, problem, issue
Question/ answer	A question is posed at the beginning, and the author answers the question in the course of the text.	answer, it could be that, one may conclude, perhaps, problem, question, solution, the best estimate, how, what, when, who, why

Note: Besides using the clue words to identify text structure, students can also analyze a chapter or a stanza and determine how it fits into the overall text structure.

Components of informational text

There are several tools authors use to help organize and support the central idea of informational text. These include:

- **Table of contents.** Outline of the text with page references
- **Headings.** Bold words or phrases that separate the text by main idea
- **Diagrams and pictures.** Visual aids to support the text
- **Glossary.** Definitions of key terms used in the text
- **Index.** Page references for key terms used in the text

3. Word choice and its effect on informational text

Often, words are defined by more than just a dictionary definition. There are two methods of describing the meaning of words: denotative and connotative.

- **Denotative meaning.** This is the literal dictionary meanings of words. Although many words have multiple meanings and can function as different parts of speech, there is no hidden suggestion or symbolic meaning behind these definitions.
    - Example: A *rock* is a stone composed of some minerals; it can also refer to a genre of music.
    - Example: *Baggage* refers to personal belongings in a suitcase.

- **Connotative meaning.** This is the suggested meaning influenced by culture or personal experience. These implied meanings are figurative and subjective because of the emotions or associations attached to them by each reader or writer. An author often uses words with positive, negative, or neutral connotations to communicate tone and mood.

  – Example: *Rock* can refer to someone who is always there for you and who you can rely on, as in *she was my **rock** during the difficult time in my life*. This word has a positive connotation in this example.

  – Example: *Baggage* has a negative connotation as it can refer to past experiences that are considered a burden, as in *he's carrying a lot of **baggage** to this situation*.

Example question

Read the paragraph below and identify how the words *electric current* and *charging* are used in the paragraph.

She felt as if her excitement was charging the air, sending an electric current throughout the atmosphere as she dashed through the monumental entryway of her new workplace. Those around her zoomed past her, only concerned with being prompt to their own jobs.

A. Connotative to set the tone for excitement

B. Denotative to understand the meaning of the words

C. Simile to compare two things

D. Hyperbole to exaggerate

Correct Answer: A

In the paragraph, the words *electric current* and *charging* are used to show an excited and heightened mood. The meaning of these words in the paragraph is connotative or implied. Simile and hyperbole are not used in the paragraph.

4. Rhetorical devices

Point of view

Understanding the author's point of view is an integral part of learning to write. Like forms of writing, students should consider audience and purpose when deciding from what point of view to write. Informational text is typically written in third-person point of view.

Point of View	Description
First person	A narrator in the story recounts his or her perspective, experience, or impressions. The pronouns *I*, *we*, *me*, *us*, are used in the text.
Second person	The story is written from the perspective of *you*. This style is rarely used.
Third person objective	The narrator remains a detached observer, telling only the action and dialogue.

Point of View	Description
Third person limited omniscient	The narrator tells the story from the viewpoint of one character in the story.
Third person omniscient	The narrator has unlimited knowledge and can describe every character's thoughts and interpret their behaviors.

5. Audience and purpose

Rhetorical devices are techniques that authors use to convey meaning that creates an effect on the reader and can be placed into one of the following categories:

1. **Ethos**. Appeals to ethics by referencing the author's credibility

2. **Pathos**. Appeals to emotions by creating an emotional response to the topic

3. **Logos**. Appeals to logic using reasons and facts.

Semantic and syntactic structures, imagery, and diction

Analysis of text requires students to understand semantic and syntactic structures, imagery and diction. These elements of text can help students derive complex meaning from text.

Attribute	Definition	Classroom Scenario
Semantic structures	Semantics is the study of meaning in language.	A teacher would like students to determine the connotative meaning of words. She writes the following sentences on the board and asks students to analyze the meaning of the word *black*. *Black and white.* *The future is black.*
Syntactic structures	Grammatical/ sentence structure	A teacher would like to illustrate how syntax can help the reader determine emotion in a text. She asks students to analyze repetition and sentence length. In groups, students try to determine the meaning of a repetitive syntactic structure and change in sentence length (e.g., from long to short sentences).
Imagery	Appealing to a reader's senses by using descriptive, sensory language	Students are asked to write a paragraph describing an experience in which they felt scared. To appeal to the reader's senses, one student writes the following sentences: *"The room was dark and cold."*
Diction	The style of speaking and writing; the choice of words	The teacher instructs students on informal and formal diction. She asks students to write on one distinct topic in two different ways. She shows the following sentences to the class to illustrate the difference: Formal: I am not optimistic about this new opportunity. Informal: I'm not cool with this new situation.

6. Written arguments

Argumentative writing requires students to understand the essential parts of an argument—claim, counterclaim, the reasons, and evidence.

- **Claim.** A claim argues or suggests something to the reader.
- **Counterclaim.** A counterclaim is a response to a claim.
- **Reasons.** Reasons are statements that provide explanations or justifications.
- **Evidence.** Evidence is information that supports an argument.

Logical fallacies

Fallacies are common errors in reasoning that undermine the logic of an argument. In addition to understanding the essential parts of an argument, students must also understand logical fallacies to determine if the argument is valid.

Common Logical Failures

Fallacy	Description	Example
Slippery slope	Asserting that one small action or step can trigger a chain of events	Allowing people to drink before the age of 21 can lead to drug abuse and death.
Bandwagon	Using popularity to validate an argument.	Everyone is doing it, so we should, too.
The strawman	Oversimplifying an argument.	This law will solve all of our problems.
The hasty generalization	Jumping to conclusions based on insufficient evidence	Private school kids get into more trouble than public school kids.

7. Media and digital literacy

Media literacy is being able to identify different types of media and understand the messages conveyed. It is important to help students separate the noise from valid messages. Start by modeling metacogntion strategies to evaluate the piece. Then, guide the whole class in evaluating the media's message. Carefully observe students as they practice independently or in small groups. These key questions will help students objectively evaluate a message:

- Who created the message?
- Who is the intended audience?
- Who might benefit from the message?
- Who might be harmed by the message?
- What techniques were used to draw the audience in?
- What opinions were expressed?
- What facts supported non-opinion statements?

- How is the message communicated?

- How does personal experience affect interpretation?

- How could the message be misinterpreted?

- Are alternate points of view acknowledged?

Test Tip

Digital news articles can be an effective tool because they contain print, audio, and video content.

Bias in media

Several methods can add bias to news media reports. Sometimes, these can be difficult to detect. Teachers must help students identify these biases. Below is a list of several obscure methods media outlets use to present biased news reports (Johnson, 2016).

Bias	Explanation
Bias through selection or omission	This is when only certain details are included in the article while other important facts are omitted.
Bias through placement	This is when specific articles are placed on the front page or web homepage to symbolize importance. Also, some facts may be deliberately added to the end of articles, which may be missed by the reader.
Bias through headlines	This is when headlines that provide a one-line summary of the report carry biased connotations.
Bias through word choice and tone	This is when words used throughout the report add positive or negative connotations. For example, "unowned cats" versus "feral cats."
Bias through photos, angles, and captions	This is when pictures capture subjects in unflattering or flattering angles. Often, these images are used along with an article to add a slant to the report.
Bias through names and titles	This is when labels are used to spin a positive or negative light onto a person or situation. For example, "ex-con" versus "served time for minor offenses."
Bias through statistics	Often, numbers can be inflated in a study to promote a particular agenda. For example, using the figure 512 versus over 500 people attended.
Bias through source control	Media outlets use numerous sources to conduct research and interviews. It is important to note whether they used a respected source of information.

Persuasive techniques

Another method to help students evaluate media messages, especially in advertising, is to teach students about the techniques used to persuade the audience. There are three basic persuasive techniques used by advertising companies to appeal to consumers:

- **Pathos.** Appeal to the emotions of the consumer

- **Logos.** Appeal to the reasonable and logical side of the consumer

- **Ethos.** Attempts to establish the credibility of the advertiser or speaker

This page intentionally left blank.

Example Questions and Answer Explanations

1. When a teacher uses a combination of literary and informational texts in classroom activities, the teacher is using a(n):

    A. Interdisciplinary approach

    B. Reader-centered approach

    C. Author-centered approach

    D. Balanced literacy approach

2. Categorize each sentence below as either denotative or connotative.

Phrase	Connotative	Denotative
He had the entire world at his fingertips.	☐	☐
The earth, together with all its countries, peoples, and natural features, is often referred to as the world.	☐	☐
The rain made the child blue because she couldn't go outside.	☐	☐
The ocean looks blue because the water absorbs red, orange, and yellow more strongly than blue.	☐	☐

3. In a periodical, an author describes a toxic work environment between the top executives and the lower-paid workers in the company. What type of allusion does the author use in the following passage?

    Once the employees found out the salaries of the CEO and other top executives were 128 times higher than regular employees, a reign of terror ensued, and the workers all but sent the bosses to the guillotine.

    A. Biblical

    B. Historical

    C. Literary

    D. Gender

4. Biographies and informational texts belong in this genre.

    A. Fiction

    B. Non-fiction

    C. Fables

    D. Historical fiction

5. A teacher in a tenth-grade English class is working with students on logical fallacies. Which of the following statements should the teacher and students analyze when examining syllogisms?

   A. *She had the world at her fingertips.*

   B. *All animals are living things. Elephants are animals. Therefore, elephants are living things.*

   C. *He nailed himself to the cross when he confessed to the crime.*

   D. *Pete produced purple petaled petunias.*

6. Which of the following is the best place to find sources that are objective, relevant, and reliable?

   A. Newspaper

   B. Government website

   C. Teach website

   D. Peer-reviewed academic journal

7. Which of the following questions would align with analyzing semantic structures in text?

   A. *Is the text grammatically correct?*

   B. *What type of imagery is used in the text?*

   C. *What is the deeper meaning of the text?*

   D. *What is the writing style used in the text?*

8. The teacher is having students draw conclusions based on information from the text. The teacher is helping students:

   A. Define words

   B. Identify structure

   C. Make inferences

   D. Avoid plagiarism

9. A teacher is going over different techniques advertising agencies use to persuade readers. The teacher and students read an ad about healthcare and its importance in the upcoming election. The ad contains a first-hand account of a woman whose son had open-heart surgery. The woman tells her story of being in cold hospital rooms waiting for doctors to come out after the surgery. It ultimately ends with a warning about one of the candidates taking healthcare away from people who need it. This type of persuasive technique uses which of the following?

   A. Pathos

   B. Logos

   C. Ethos

   D. Bias

10. A teacher wants to help students understand bias in media. After a whole-group session on bias and its uses in media, she has students work in cooperative groups. Which of the following would be the best activity to have students work on in their groups?

A. Have students work in groups to make a poster about the dangers of bias in the media and how it negatively affects readers.

B. Have students read a section in the textbook and outline bias in publications.

C. Have students read a preidentified group of articles, locate areas of biased and nonbiased information in the articles, and discuss them as a group.

D. Have students write a group research paper about how bias has been detrimental to the country during elections.

Number	Answer	Explanation
1.	D	A balanced literary approach in the classroom is effective because it involves literary and informational text. You may be tempted to choose interdisciplinary; however, interdisciplinary means using other content areas like social science, English, and science together to teach a unit. Reader-centered and author-centered do not fit here.

| 2. | See chart | |

Phrase	Connotative	Denotative
He had the entire world at his fingertips.	x	
The earth, together with all of its countries, peoples, and natural features is often referred to as the world.		x
The rain made the child blue because she couldn't go outside.	x	
The ocean looks blue because red, orange and yellow are absorbed more strongly by water than blue.		x

The emotions and associations connected to a word are known as its **connotative** meaning. The dictionary definition of a word is denotative.

Quick Tip

Think **d**enotative and **d**ictionary **d**efinition.

Number	Answer	Explanation
3.	B	This is a historical reference to the French Revolution and the Reign of Terror. During this time, common people in France engaged in an uprising, detained the nobles, and sent them to the guillotine to be beheaded.
4.	B	Informational text is considered nonfiction because it informs the reader about the natural or social world.
5.	B	A syllogism is a three-part logical argument based on deductive reasoning, combining two premises to arrive at a conclusion. Therefore, answer choice B is a syllogism. Answer A is an idiom. Answer B is an allusion (biblical). Answer D is an alliteration.

Number	Answer	Explanation
6.	D	A peer-reviewed academic journal is always the best place to find information. While government websites have relevant information, select the peer-reviewed academic journal to ensure objectivity.
7.	C	If students analyze semantic text structures, they are looking for the intended meaning of the language the author uses. Remember that **semantic** refers to word meaning, and **syntactic** refers to grammar. Answer choice C is the only question that relates to the meaning of the text.
8.	C	An inference is a conclusion based on evidence or reasoning from the text. This is an essential process for reading comprehension.
9.	A	Using pathos attempts to appeal to the emotional side of the audience. This scenario clearly outlines an emotional situation. Therefore, pathos is the best answer here.
10.	C	Answer choice C is the only answer choice where students apply their knowledge of bias and identify it in the real world. Answer choices A and D are essentially the same and do not require students to apply their knowledge in identifying bias. In these two answer choices, students simply define what bias is. Reading the textbook, as in answer choice B, is ineffective for this situation.

II. Language Use and Vocabulary

II. Language Use and Vocabulary

1. Standard English grammar, usage, syntax, and mechanics

2. Affixes, context, and syntax

3. Print and digital reference materials

4. Dialect and diction across regions, cultural groups, and time periods

5. Research-based approaches for supporting language acquisition and vocabulary development for diverse learners

1. Standard English grammar, usage, syntax, and mechanics

To be an effective secondary English instructor, you must have a command of standard English grammar and usage. You will encounter grammar questions on this exam.

Verbs

Verbs are words used to describe **actions** or states, and they form the main part of the predicate of the sentence. Some common examples of verbs include *to be, to think, to take, to come, to see, to have, to do, to go,* and *to make.* Verbs can be regular or irregular, and depending on their status, they will be conjugated differently. For example, to show the past tense of a regular verb, we add the *-ed* ending (e.g., called).

Standard verb forms

There are five main forms of verbs: simple or base form, third-person singular present (also called *s* form), past tense form, *-ing* form, and past participle form. Typically, verb form is assessed on the exam with questions that test your ability to spot and correct errors in incorrect form use.

Verb form	Definition	Example
Simple or base form	The verb's simple form is the present tense.	I *dance* at the wedding. The boys *walk* to school. I *buy* clothes at my favorite store.
Third person singular present (s form)	Most verbs in English form the third-person singular by adding *-s* or *-es* to the simple or base form of the verb. These actions are in the present tense.	She *dances* after school. The boy *walks* to school. The child *watches* TV.
Past tense form	This is the basic past tense of the verb. For regular verbs, add -ed to the root form of the verb (or just -d if the root form already ends in an e). However, some past tense verbs are irregular and do not have -ed attached to the end.	She *danced* in yesterday's competition. The kids *watched* the ball game last night. The contest *was* held in the auditorium. The workers *built* the house quickly.

Verb form	Definition	Example
-ing form	A verb ending in *-ing* is either a present participle or a gerund. These two forms look identical. The difference is in their functions in a sentence.	**Present participle:** • He is *painting* in class. • She was *dancing* in the street. • I see the kids *playing* in the yard. **Gerund** – When the verb is the subject and functions as a noun. • *Painting* is a fun activity. • *Eating* dirt is a bad idea. • *Walking* to school is easier than driving.
Past participle form	The past participle is also used with *had* or *have* to form the past perfect tense.	I *have driven* that route before. She *had tried* to call him before the party. I *have completed* my homework.

Example question

Choose the option that corrects an error in the underlined portion(s). If no error exists, choose "No change is necessary."

She <u>was</u> unable to pick up her prescription after work. She <u>drive</u> as fast as she <u>could and</u> still didn't make it.
    A   B   C

A. were

B. drove

C. could, and

D. No change is necessary.

Correct Answer: B

In this case, the verb *drive* is not the proper verb form. This sentence is past tense. Therefore, *drive* should be changed to *drove*.

Inappropriate shifts in verb tense

Writing should maintain a consistent verb tense throughout a sentence or paragraph. For example, if a sentence is written in the present tense, it should not suddenly shift to the past tense. Similarly, if a sentence or paragraph begins in the past tense, it should remain in the past tense throughout the entire work. Typically, verb form is assessed on the exam with questions that test your ability to spot and correct errors in maintaining consistent verb tense throughout the sentence or paragraph.

Choose the option that corrects an error in the underlined portion(s). If no error exists, choose "No change is necessary."

She drove <u>quickly</u> and still didn't make it. The professor <u>locks</u> her <u>out because</u> she was five minutes late.
            A   B   C

- A. quick
- B. locked
- C. out, because
- D. No change is necessary.

Correct Answer: B

In this case, the verb *locks* does not match the verb tense of the rest of the sentence. This sentence is past tense. Therefore, *locks* should be changed to *locked*. The adverb *quickly* is used correctly. For answer choice C, you should not use a comma before the word *because*.

Subject-verb agreement

Subject-verb agreement simply means the subject and verb must agree in number. This means both the subject and verb need to be singular or both need to be plural.

Example:

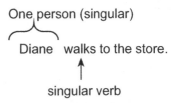

Diane   walks to the store.

singular verb

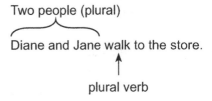

Diane and Jane walk to the store.

plural verb

> **Test Tip**
>
> Test makers will often write items using sneaky prepositional phrases, making it difficult to locate the subject.
>
> **Incorrect:**
>
> The use of cell phones are prohibited.
>
> You may think this sentence is grammatically correct because *cell phones* comes before the verb *are*.
>
> However, the subject in this sentence is *the use*. The phrase *cell phones* is the prepositional phrase, not the subject.
>
> **Correct:**
>
> The <u>use</u> of cell phones <u>is</u> prohibited.

Example question

Choose the option that corrects an error in the underlined portion(s). If no error exists, choose "No change is necessary."

The use of <u>cellphones and</u> other recording devices <u>are</u> banned <u>from</u> the museum.
                   A   B   C

A. cellphones, and

B. is

C. out because

D. No change is necessary.

Correct Answer: B

In this case, the subject is *the use* (singular). The phrase *of cellphones and other recording devices* is plural, but it is not the subject. Instead, it is a prepositional phrase. You can remove the prepositional phrase, and the sentence would read: The use *is* prohibited.

Test Tip

Another way this is presented is when using *neither* and *nor*, and *either* and *or*. These words make the subject of the sentence singular, as in the following example.

Neither Jane nor Diane walks to the store.

In this case, *neither* separates each subject as one.

The following test question is how this may be presented on the exam.

Example question

Choose the option that corrects an error in the underlined portion(s). If no error exists, choose "No change is necessary."

Either the dog <u>or</u> the cat <u>have</u> to be boarded while we are on <u>vacation; we</u> cannot take both.
                  A   B   C

A. nor

B. has

C. vacation, we

D. No change is necessary.

Correct Answer: B

The word *either* makes each subject its own singular noun. Therefore, the dog *has* to be boarded or the cat *has* to be boarded.

Phrasal verbs

These phrases combine verbs and participles, usually prepositions or adverbs, to create a whole new meaning or multiple meanings. Let's look at examples of phrasal verbs with *stand*.

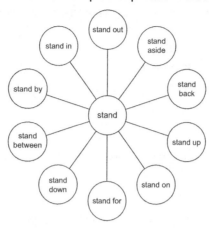

Example question

Ms. Evans notices that in most students' writing samples, the students in her 6th grade ELA class frequently use adjectives where they should use adverbs. She decides that the next time they read, she will have them look up each word in the dictionary and copy it down. Is this an effective way to correct this usage error?

A. Yes. Students would benefit from identifying part of speech for each word. Repeated practice is always effective.

B. No. She should ask students to watch a video about parts of speech. Then, the students can try the activity again.

C. Yes. Using a dictionary should be the main mode of identifying parts of speech.

D. No. A better approach would be to conduct a detailed whole-group lesson on the differences between adjectives and adverbs and provide guided practice followed by independent practice

Correct Answer: D

Because this is a whole-class issue, a whole-group lesson followed by guided and individual practice is the best approach. The correct answer is D.

Pronoun antecedent agreement

Pronoun antecedent agreement simply means that the pronoun used in the sentence agrees with the antecedent in the sentence.

First, distinguish between a pronoun and an antecedent by looking at the sentence below.

My *teacher* was excited to learn that three of *her* students were accepted to Ivy League colleges.

Antecedent   Pronoun

In the case above, the pronoun, *her*, matches the antecedent, *teacher*.

However, things get complicated when the test makers present the pronouns *they*, *them*, or *their* in a sentence.

Incorrect:

One person (singular)

When a student comes to see me, <u>they</u> usually want to discuss extra credit.

Plural pronoun

The sentence above is incorrect because the plural pronoun, *they*, disagrees with the singular noun in the subject, *student*.

Correct:

When <u>students</u> come to see me, <u>they</u> usually want to discuss extra credit.

Example question

Choose the option that corrects an error in the underlined portion(s). If no error exists, choose "No change is necessary."

The board of directors had <u>their</u> <u>meeting and</u> decided to postpone the event until after the <u>holidays</u>.

                           A   B   C

A. its

B. meeting, and

C. Holidays

D. No change is necessary.

Correct Answer: A

In this case, there is a sneaky prepositional phrase and a collective noun to navigate. *The board* is a collective noun and therefore singular. To have pronoun antecedent agreement, the pronoun *its* is appropriate for the singular *board*. The phrase *of directors* is a prepositional phrase and can be taken out. Then the sentence would read: *The board had its meeting.*

In answer choice B, there is no need for the comma + conjunction because the *and* is only separating a dependent and independent clause, so the conjunction *and* by itself is correct. Finally, the term *holidays* is not a proper noun and does not need to be capitalized.

Example question

Choose the option that corrects an error in the underlined portion(s). If no error exists, choose "No change is necessary."

<u>A student should only go to their locker</u> before school, during lunch, or after school.

A. Students should only go their locker

B. A student should go to their lockers

C. Students should only go to their lockers

D. No change is necessary.

Correct Answer: C

The way the sentence is written, the subject is singular (a student), and the pronoun is plural (their). Therefore, the best thing to do is change the subject to plural (students). Also, because we have multiple students, there are multiple lockers. Therefore, *locker* should be changed to a plural noun as well. Otherwise, it reads as though there are multiple students using one locker.

Pronoun references

Sometimes it is unclear to what antecedent the pronoun is referring. In that case, you will be tasked to identify that in a sentence.

Incorrect:

My sister brought her dog on the road trip, and she chewed the seats.

There are two antecedents in this sentence, and it is unclear who the pronoun *she* is referring to. Is *she* referring to the sister or the dog?

Correct:

My sister brought her dog on the road trip, and the dog chewed the seats.

In this sentence, it is clear that the dog, not the sister, chewed the seats.

Pronoun case forms (e.g., subjective, objective, possessive)

Just like verbs, pronouns have cases. Pronouns can be either subjective (occurring in the subject of the sentence), objective (occurring as the direct object in the predicate of the sentence), or possessive (showing ownership). The following are examples of each pronoun case.

Subject Pronouns	Examples
I	**She** went to the store to buy milk.
he	↑
she	**She** is the subject of the sentence and therefore a subjective pronoun.
they	**They** rode bikes to school.
we	↑
you	**They** is the subject of the sentence and therefore a subjective pronoun.
who	

Object Pronouns	Examples
me	Jane went to the store to buy **him** some clothes.
him	↑
her	The pronoun **him** is the direct object of the sentence and therefore the objective pronoun.
them	Sally came over to the house to see **me**.
us	↑
you	The pronoun **me** is the direct object of the sentence and therefore the objective pronoun.
whom	

Possessive Pronouns	Examples
my	She went to get **her** clothes from the house.
his	↑
her	The pronoun **her** is the possessive pronoun.
their	We realized it was **their** car in the parking lot.
our	↑
your	The pronoun **their** is the possessive pronoun.
whose	

Example question

Choose the option that corrects an error in the underlined portion(s). If no error exists, choose "No change is necessary."

I was excited when the <u>university</u> professor <u>came</u> over to speak with my son <u>and I</u>.
                        A   B   C

A. University

B. come

C. and me.

D. No change is necessary.

Correct Answer: C

A lot of people have difficulty spotting this error. In fact, many people erroneously think that using the pronoun *I* in this way is grammatically correct. However, *I* is a subject pronoun. In the case above, *I* is used incorrectly as a direct object pronoun. The appropriate pronoun should be *me*.

Example question

Choose the option that corrects an error in the underlined portion(s). If no error exists, choose "No change is necessary."

Her and I were very close when we were younger, but we grew apart when I moved away.
A   B   C

- A. She
- B. and me
- C. younger but
- D. No change is necessary.

Correct Answer: A

In this case, the object pronoun, *her*, is used erroneously as a subject pronoun. If I take out the *I* in the sentence, it reads:

Her was very close…

It should be:

She was very close…

Example question

Choose the option that corrects an error in the underlined portion(s). If no error exists, choose "No change is necessary."

My mother said I can go to the play with whoever I want.

- A. with whomever
- B. with whosever
- C. with who
- D. No change is necessary.

Correct Answer: A

Remember, *who* is a subject pronoun, and *whom* is an object pronoun. In this case, the subject is *I*, as in "I can go with…" Therefore, an object pronoun (*whomever*) is needed.

Test Tip

If you are stuck on *who* vs. *whom*, remember that *whom* follows the prepositions *with* and *of*. So, if you see *with* or *of*, whom is the correct pronoun. Another trick is to answer the question. In the case above, the speaker can go with *whomever* because she can go with *him*, *her*, or *them*. These are all direct object pronouns and match *whom*.

Adjectives and adverbs

Adjectives modify or describe nouns or pronouns. They are either attributive adjectives (before the noun) or predicate adjectives (after a verb of being):

Example:

The <u>brave</u> girl rescued her mom from the burning home. She is a hero.

In this case, the adjective—brave—is describing the noun—girl.

Example:

The girl is <u>brave</u>.

In this case, the adjective—brave—is describing the noun—girl.

Adverbs modify or describe **verbs, adverbs, or adjectives**.

Example:

The girl <u>bravely</u> rescued her mom from the burning home. She acted <u>heroically</u>.

Common adjective-adverb combinations are listed in the table that follows. Notice that there are some common exceptions to the *-ly* pattern.

Quick Tip

Many times, adding an *ly, ally* or *i + ly* to an adjective, forms an adverb:

- brave + ly = bravely
  She **bravely walked** into battle.

- beautiful + ly = beautifully
  She **wrote** her name **beautifully** on the paper.

- gentle + ly = gently (drop the e)
  She **pets** the sick dog **gently** on the head.

- easy + i + ly = easily (drop the y and add the i to words that end in y)
  She **worked** through the math problems **easily**.

Adjectives	Adverbs
good	well
fast, quick	fast, quickly
slow, deliberate, lethargic	slowly, deliberately, lethargically
awkward	awkwardly
needless	needlessly
super, superb	superbly
responsible	responsibly
near, far	nearly, far

Choose the option that corrects an error in the underlined portion(s). If no error exists, choose "No change is necessary."

She was moving along <u>slow because</u> she had not driven down that road before.

- A. slow, because
- B. slowly because
- C. slowly, because
- D. No change is necessary.

Correct Answer: B

In this case, the adverb is needed because it is describing the verb *moving*. Also, a comma is not needed between *slowly* and *because*.

Comparative and superlative degree forms

Comparatives and superlatives compare things. *Comparatives* compare two things, while *superlatives* compare three or more things.

Example:

Steve is **better** than Joe at baseball.

The word <u>better</u> is a comparative. It compares only two things.

Example:

Out of everyone in the class, Jody is the **tallest**.

The word *tallest* is a superlative. It compares three or more things.

Example question

Choose the option that corrects an error in the underlined portion(s). If no error exists, choose "No change is necessary."

Of all the hundreds of dresses in the store, Kelly liked the red sequin dress <u>more</u>.

- A. most
- B. better
- C. more better
- D. No change is necessary.

Correct Answer: A

Because there are more than two dresses being compared, the comparative *more* is incorrect and should be replaced with the superlative *most*.

Test Tip

When answering these questions, pay attention to words like *more* and *most* and *better* and *best*. People often use these incorrectly in everyday speech.

Quick Tip

It is important to be aware that when comparing two things, use the subjective pronoun NOT the objective pronoun.

Incorrect:

John is taller than **me.**

Correct:

John is taller than **I.**

The reason you do not use *me* is because the sentence is really saying:

John is taller than **I am tall.**

II. LANGUAGE USE AND VOCABULARY

Activity – Identify errors in student writing samples.

Below are student samples of writing with corrections. Identify the type of skill in each error: subject-verb agreement, misplaced modifier, adverbs-adjectives, parallel structure, pronoun shift, or pronoun-antecedent agreement.

	Sample	Correction	Skill
1.	When I go to school, I make sure my backpack has paper, pencils, and that I brought my lunch.	When I go to school, I make sure my backpack has my paper, pencils, and lunch.	
2.	My soccer team have practice at 4 pm.	My soccer team has practice at 4 pm.	
3.	The band is holding a fundraiser this weekend to buy their new uniforms.	The band is holding a fundraiser this weekend to buy its new uniforms.	
4.	When I ordered a new bike, I forgot that you have to specify which color you want, so I ended up with pink.	When I ordered a new bike, I forgot that I have to specify which color I want, so I ended up with pink.	
5.	I saw a dollar walking down the street.	While walking down the street, I saw a dollar.	
6.	When my dad heard me scream, he ran quick into the room to help me.	When my dad heard me scream, he ran quickly into the room to help me.	
7.	I am doing good.	I am doing well.	
8.	The professor returned the exam with a smile.	The professor, who was smiling, returned the exam.	
9.	The stack of books are about to fall off the table.	The stack of books is about to fall off the table.	
10.	The teacher asked us to write our essays in a way that it is organized, and he also would like more details.	The teacher asked us to write our essays in an organized and detailed way.	

Answer key: 1. parallel structure, 2. subject-verb agreement, 3. pronoun-antecedent agreement, 4. pronoun shift, 5. misplaced modifier, 6. adjective-adverb, 7. adjective-adverb, 8. misplaced modifier, 9. subject-verb agreement, 10 parallel structure.

Modifiers

A misplaced modifier is a word, phrase, or clause improperly separated from the word it modifies or describes. The separation causes an error that makes the sentence confusing.

Incorrect:

Yolanda realized too late that it was a mistake to walk the neighbor's dog in high heels.

In this sentence, the phrase *in high heels* modifies *the neighbor's dog*. The dog is not in high heels; Yolanda is.

Correct:

Yolanda realized too late that she shouldn't have worn high heels while walking the neighbor's dog.

To correct the error, rearrange the sentence so the modifying clause is close to the word it should modify.

Example question

Choose the sentence in which the modifiers are correctly placed.

    A. While attending the political town hall, new laws were opposed by demonstrators that would negatively impact the city.

    B. New laws were opposed by demonstrators while attending the political town hall that would negatively impact the city.

    C. While attending the political town hall, demonstrators staged a sit-in to oppose a new law that would negatively impact the city.

    D. New laws that would negatively impact the city were opposed while attending the political town hall by demonstrators.

Correct Answer: C

In this test item, the modifier is *while attending the political town hall*. In choice A, *while attending the political town hall* is modifying *new laws*. That makes it sound like the new laws are attending the town hall. In choice B, *while attending the political town hall* is modifying *negatively impact the city*, making it sound like the town hall would negatively impact the city. In choice D, *while attending the political town hall* is modifying *new laws*, making it sound like the new laws are attending the town hall. Notice that in choice C, the modifier *while attending the political town tall* is modifying the demonstrators.

Quick Tip

Place the modifier next to the portion of the sentence it is modifying.

The demonstrators are attending the town hall.

While attending the political town hall, demonstrators staged a sit-in to oppose a new law that would negatively impact the city.

Parallelism

Parallelism refers to the same pattern of words or repetition of a chosen grammatical form within a sentence. Parallel structure is when a sentence follows the same grammatical pattern.

Incorrect:

The superintendent was delighted to see the crew had finished the job, cleaned up the site, and some were organizing the tools.

Correct:

The superintendent was delighted to see the crew had finished the job, cleaned up the site, and organized the tools.

Notice the list in the correct example is parallel; the verbs are all past tense and are followed by nouns.

Choose the correct word or phrase that provides parallel structure to the sentence.

After the party, we cleaned the patio, swept the stairs, washed the dishes, and _____ to bed.

    A. were finally able to go

    B. after went

    C. was going

    D. went

Correct Answer: D

In the list in the sentence, there are past tense verbs followed by noun(s). *Were finally able to, after went*, and *was going* break the parallel structure in the sentence. The word *went* is most appropriate.

Test Tip

Using the fewest words to convey an idea in writing is most effective. If there is an answer choice that is shorter than the others and is grammatically correct, then it is most likely the correct answer.

Orthography

Orthography refers to the conventional spelling of words and the rules associated with spelling. Remember, there are exceptions to these rules.

- Use *i* before *e*, except after *c*, or when sounding like *a* as *neighbor* and *weight*.

- Drop the final *e* when adding a suffix that starts with a vowel, but not when adding a suffix starting with a consonant.

- Change the final *y* to *i* before adding a suffix unless the suffix begins with *i*.

- Double a final single consonant before adding a suffix when the word ends with a single vowel followed by a single consonant and when the consonant ends an accented syllable or a one-syllable word.

- The letter *q* is typically followed by the letter *u*.

- To change a word that ends with a *y* to be plural, change the *y* to *i* and add *es*.

Standard spelling conventions

There are an infinite number of spelling patterns that could be presented on the exam. Spelling is sometimes assessed by using commonly confused words.

Choose the option that corrects an error in the underlined portion(s). If no error exists, choose "No change is necessary."

We are looking <u>forward</u> to receiving the <u>funds, but</u> we need some <u>advise</u> on how to spend them.
            A   B   C

A. forwards

B. funds but

C. advice

D. No change is necessary.

Correct Answer: C

The correct word here is *advice*, the noun. *Advise*, as used in the original sentence, is a verb.

Standard punctuation – Commas

No other punctuation mark is misused as often as the comma. Its use in items in a series is also hotly debated right now. The traditional Oxford comma separates items in a series of three items or more, including the item before the coordinating conjunction.

Examples:

I went to the store to buy milk, eggs, cheese, and bread.

I went to the store to buy milk, eggs, cheese and bread.

In the first example, the Oxford comma is used before *and* in the sentence; in the second example, the Oxford comma is not used before *and* in the sentence. It is important to understand that you will not be asked on a grammar test to choose between using the Oxford comma and not using the Oxford comma because both are considered correct. The choice is a stylistic one.

Comma Usage Rules

Usage	Example
After an introductory word, phrase, or clause	However, he did not follow the rules.
To separate a dependent clause from an independent clause when the dependent clause comes first	When he turned in his homework a day late, the teacher tossed it in the garbage.
Before a coordinating conjunction to separate two independent clauses	I went to my interview today, and I think it went really well.
To separate items in a series of three items or more	The girl went shopping for school supplies such as notebooks, pens, pencils, highlighters, and binders.
To separate two consecutive adjectives	The tall, muscular girl was the star of the basketball team.
On both sides of nonessential words, phrases, or clauses	The teacher, who had little experience, assigned reading from a banned book.

Usage	Example
To set off someone's name or title	Excuse me, Alyssa, but I need to take this call.
To separate the day, month, and year in a date (and after the year if it is part of a sentence)	June 14, 1969, is my birthdate.
To separate a city from a state	I am from Dunedin, Florida.
To introduce or separate a quote	She screamed, "I hate you!" "Why," I asked, "do you hate me?"
Before the end quotation mark if the quote is followed by an attribution such as he said	"I can't stand it anymore," he said.
To separate contrasting parts of a sentence	That is my drink, not yours.

Example question

Choose the option that corrects an error in the underlined portion(s). If no error exists, choose "No change is necessary."

After the movie, she said "I don't understand why there is always so much violence in film."
                  A   B   C

   A. said, "I don't

   B. their

   C. film".

   D. No change is necessary.

Correct Answer: A

A comma is needed to separate a quote in a sentence. Therefore, the comma must be added here.

Standard punctuation – Semicolons

Semicolons join two independent clauses that are related. Semicolons are alternatives to a period or comma conjunction.

Examples:

I needed to go to the store; I was almost out of milk, egg, cheese, and bread.

He knew he would be punished for skipping school; he did it anyway.

In both examples above, there are two independent clauses joined by the semicolon. This is the only way to use a semicolon.

Choose the option that corrects an error in the underlined portion(s). If no error exists, choose "No change is necessary."

We tried to <u>build</u> the house on our <u>own; but</u> we soon realized we <u>needed</u> help.
            A   B   C

A. built

B. own, but

C. need

D. No change is necessary.

Correct Answer: B

You do not use a semicolon and a coordinating conjunction together. Never use a semicolon before coordinating conjunctions (*for, and, nor, but, or, yet, so*) in a sentence.

Standard punctuation – Colons

Colons are used to separate an independent clause and a list. Colons can also be used to separate an independent clause and an independent clause or dependent clause that elaborates, restates, explains, or defines.

Example:

I brought all the necessities to the campsite: tent, food, fishing pole, and tackle.

Notice that the clause, *I brought all the necessities to the campsite*, is a sentence—an independent clause. Therefore, the colon is used correctly.

Example:

We decided to focus on the most important thing: increasing student achievement.

The dependent clause, which is *increasing student achievement*, defines what the most important thing is.

Example:

I had lunch with the president of the university: Dr. Cunningham.

Here you have an independent clause followed by the name of the person mentioned in the first clause. Therefore, the colon is appropriate.

Example question

Choose the option that corrects an error in the underlined portion(s). If no error exists, choose "No change is necessary."

We were waiting on several of our <u>items such as: books, scissors, and pencils.</u>

A. items: books, scissors, and pencils.

B. Items like our: books, scissors, and pencils.

C. items, books, scissors, and pencils.

D. No change is necessary.

Correct Answer: A

Correct use of a colon requires an independent clause before the colon and a list or a definition after the colon. The phrase *such as* should be removed from the sentence. Doing so creates an independent clause before the colon.

Standard punctuation – Apostrophe

There are two main reasons to use apostrophes:

1. To form a contraction such as do + not = don't. In this case, the apostrophe replaces or stands in for the letter that is taken out when the words are combined.

2. To show possession. When the noun is singular or plural but does not end in **s**, add **'s** to show possession. When the noun is singular or plural but does end in **s**, add the apostrophe **after the s** to show possession.

Example:

Please bring **Lisa's** book when you come to class tomorrow.

Lisa is a singular proper noun (there is only one Lisa here); therefore, the **'s** is appropriate.

Example:

We will be going to the **women's** soccer tournament on Wednesday.

Women is a plural noun that does NOT end in s; therefore, the **'s** is appropriate.

Example:

Please bring all the **girls'** books when you come to class tomorrow.

Girls is a plural noun that ends in s; therefore, the **s'** is appropriate.

Example:

We will be going to the **ladies'** luncheon on Friday.

Ladies is plural and ends in -s, and the ladies own the luncheon. Therefore, the **s'** is appropriate.

Example question

Choose the option that corrects an error in the underlined portion(s). If no error exists, choose "No change is necessary."

I am not excited about <u>tomorrows</u> meeting.

   A. tomorrow

   B. tomorrow's

   C. tomorrows'

   D. No change is necessary.

Correct Answer: B

In cases like this, the meeting belongs to *tomorrow*. Therefore, it should be *tomorrow's meeting*.

Standard capitalization

Capitalization for standard English follows a few basic rules.

Rule one:	Always capitalize the first word of a sentence.

The key here is to recognize where the sentences start and stop. For example, semicolons connect two sentences together as one; therefore, they do not need capitalization except at the beginning (unless the second sentence starts with a proper noun).

Example:

Capitalization can be tricky; there are several rules.

Notice that the **C** in *capitalization* is capitalized, but the **t** in *there* is not.

Rule two:	Always capitalize proper nouns and their titles as well as the abbreviations of these.

Names of specific people and places are capitalized.

Example:

During the Civil War, President Abraham Lincoln was president of the United States.

Civil War is a specific name of a war. *President* is the title of *Abraham Lincoln* in the subject. However, *president* is a common noun in the predicate.

Example:

Today, Congress passed a law banning congressional pay raises even though the Senate had to vote on it three times.

Congress and *Senate* are, in this case, names.

Rule three:	Capitalize the main words in a multiword title.

Here, the emphasis is also on what **not** to capitalize: articles (other than the first word), conjunctions, and prepositions.

Examples:

He works at the Federal Bureau of Investigation in Washington, DC.

Poe's *Tales of Mystery and Imagination* is one of my favorite collections.

Notice that the articles and prepositions—is, in, of, and—are not capitalized in the title.

Example question

Choose the option that corrects an error in the underlined portion(s). If no error exists, choose "No change is necessary."

I wait every year for the Fall; it's my favorite holiday.

- A. fall; it's
- B. Fall, its
- C. fall, its
- D. No change is necessary.

Correct Answer: A

The seasons are not capitalized unless they are attached to a proper noun, as in the annual Fall Festival or Winter Dance. Also, in this question, *it's* is the proper conjunction for *it is*. Finally, the semicolon is used correctly, separating two independent clauses.

Caution

On the test, you will often be assessed on your ability to identify when NOT to capitalize, like this example question.

Effective writers use a mix of compound and complex sentences to illustrate sentence variety, which adds vibrancy and interest to text. You will see questions on the exam about helping students increase their writing skills by using sentence variety.

Sentence Type	Explanation	Example
Simple sentence	Consists of one **independent** clause	I went to the store.
Compound sentence	Consists of **two independent** clauses. Ensure that there is a comma between two independent clauses in a compound sentence. The comma should be followed by a coordinating conjunction (**FANBOYS**)	I went to the store, and I bought milk.
Complex sentence	Consists of an independent clause and a dependent clause. When the sentence starts with a dependent clause, a comma is needed after the clause.	When I went to the store, I bought milk.
Compound complex sentence	Consists of at least two independent clauses and at least one dependent clause.	When I went to the store, I bought milk, and I bought cheese.

Identifying independent and dependent clauses

The best approach to this part of the assessment is understanding the difference between independent and dependent clauses.

- An **independent clause** contains a subject and a verb and expresses a complete thought. An independent clause can stand on its own as a sentence.

- A **dependent clause** contains a noun and a verb but does not express a complete thought. A dependent clause cannot be a sentence on its own.

Example:

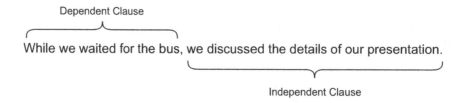

Dependent Clause

While we waited for the bus, we discussed the details of our presentation.

Independent Clause

Fragments

Dependent clauses, without the independent clause in a sentence, are fragments. Fragments are not sentences.

Incorrect:

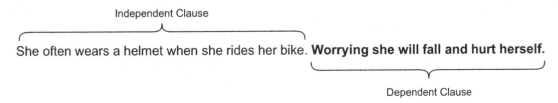

Correct:

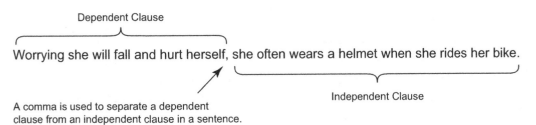

A comma is used to separate a dependent clause from an independent clause in a sentence.

Quick Tip

You can take a fragment and add it to an independent clause to make a complete sentence as long as you place a comma, separating them appropriately.

Example question

Choose the option that corrects an error in the underlined portion(s). If no error exists, choose "No change is necessary."

She is constantly checking her <u>work. Making</u> sure she didn't make any mistakes.

    A. work, making

    B. work; making

    C. work making

    D. No change is necessary.

Correct Answer: A

In this case, *Making sure she didn't make any mistakes* is a fragment; it is just the verb phrase. Therefore, it cannot be a sentence on its own as it is originally presented, making option D "No change is necessary" incorrect. In answer choice B, the semicolon is incorrect because semicolons separate two independent clauses. The clause *Making sure she didn't make any mistakes* is not an independent clause. Having no punctuation between the two clauses makes the sentence a run-on and, therefore, incorrect, eliminating answer choice C. In answer choice A, a comma between *work* and *making* is correct because the comma is separating an independent clause from a dependent clause.

Comma splice

Commas are used to separate an independent from a dependent clause. When commas are incorrectly used to separate two independent clauses, it is called a **comma splice**. Commas are NOT used to separate two independent clauses. On the exam, you will be required to identify and correct comma splices.

Incorrect:

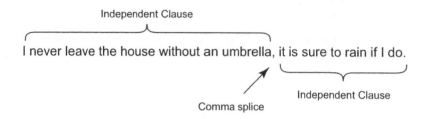

Correct:

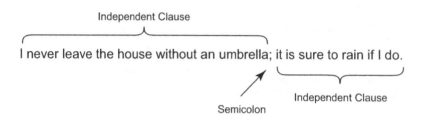

Example question

Choose the option that corrects an error in the underlined portion(s). If no error exists, choose "No change is necessary."

The teacher stood confidently to accept her <u>award, among</u> those in the audience were some of her former students.

  A. award. Among

  B. but among

  C. and among

  D. No change is necessary

Correct Answer: A

This sentence contains a comma splice, making "No change is necessary" incorrect. Removing the comma and inserting either the conjunction *but* or the conjunction *and* causes the sentence to be a run-on, eliminating choices B and C.

Run on sentences

A run-on sentence occurs when two or more independent clauses are joined incorrectly. A comma splice, as mentioned above, is a common way run-on sentences are formed. However, there are a number of ways the test presents run-on sentences. The sentences below are run-on sentences, and in all cases, they are punctuated incorrectly.

Incorrect:

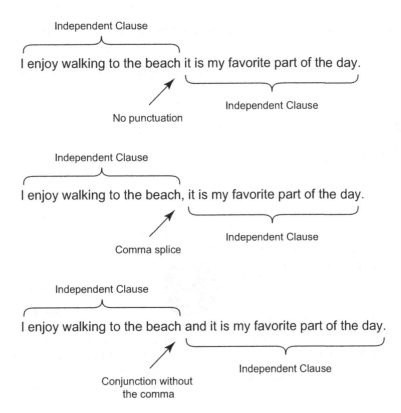

Correct:

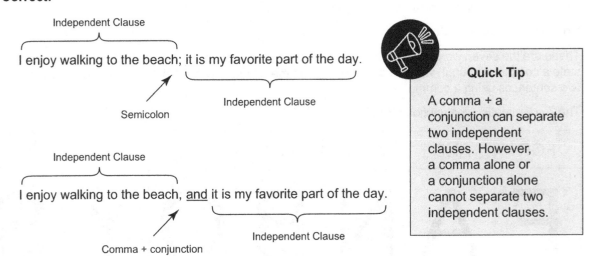

Quick Tip

A comma + a conjunction can separate two independent clauses. However, a comma alone or a conjunction alone cannot separate two independent clauses.

Choose the option that corrects an error in the underlined portion(s). If no error exists, choose "No change is necessary."

The <u>book *To Kill a Mockingbird* is</u> part of the high school English <u>curriculum but</u> many schools have
    A   B   C
banned the book.

    A. The book: *To*

    B. *Mockingbird*, is

    C. curriculum, but

    D. No change is necessary.

Correct Answer: C

This sentence, as it is presented, is a run-on sentence because there is no comma before the conjunction, *but*. This sentence contains two independent clauses:

The book, *To Kill a Mockingbird*, is part of the high school English curriculum. Many schools have banned the book.

Notice how both clauses can stand on their own as sentences. They are independent clauses; therefore, the conjunction by itself is incorrect. There needs to be a comma + conjunction as indicated in answer choice C.

Quick Tip

While conjunctions link words and groups of words, subordinating and coordinating conjunctions connect clauses (a group of words containing a subject and a verb).

Coordinating conjunctions

These are the seven words that combine two sentences (independent clauses that can stand alone as they state a complete thought) with the addition of a comma. These are the ONLY seven words used to combine two sentences using a comma.

The 7 coordinating conjunctions (FANBOYS):

FOR	AND	NOR	BUT	OR	YET	SO
F	A	N	B	O	Y	S

- A conjunction alone can separate an independent clause and a dependent clause.
- A comma + a conjunction must be used when separating two independent clauses.

Example:

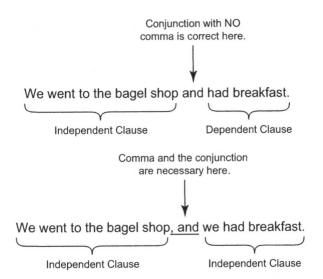

Conjunction with NO comma is correct here.

We went to the bagel shop and had breakfast.

Independent Clause   Dependent Clause

Comma and the conjunction are necessary here.

We went to the bagel shop, and we had breakfast.

Independent Clause   Independent Clause

Subordinating conjunctions

These are all the other conjunctions used to combine clauses. These commonly include:

- Since
- Because
- Although
- While
- Due
- Though
- Whenever
- When
- If
- Therefore

> ### Quick Tip
>
> **YES,** you can start sentences with subordinating conjunctions.
>
> - *While* I was watching TV, I did my homework.
> - *Since* it was cold, I wore a jacket.
> - *Whenever* I go to Canada, I stop in Seattle on the way.
> - *Because* I was on the committee, I voted on the issue.

*When a subordinating conjunction starts a sentence, a comma will always follow.

Grammatically, there are two patterns for these subordinating conjunctions:

Pattern 1

Independent Clause + Subordinating Conjunction + Clause (independent, dependent, or prepositional)

Example:

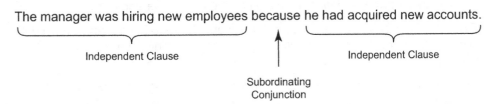

The manager was hiring new employees because he had acquired new accounts.

Independent Clause   Independent Clause

Subordinating Conjunction

Pattern 2

Subordinating Conjunction + Clause (independent, dependent, or prepositional) + Comma + Independent Clause

Example:

Because he had acquired new accounts, the manager was hiring new employees.

Subordinating Conjunction   Independent Clause   Independent Clause

Example question

Choose the option that corrects an error in the underlined portion(s). If no error exists, choose "No change is necessary."

He rarely slept because he was always traveling through different time zones.
     A   B   C

A. rare

B. slept, because

C. threw

D. No change is necessary.

Correct Answer: D

Because is a subordinating conjunction and does not need a comma before it. The way the sentence is presented originally is correct. Therefore, no change is necessary.

2. Affixes, context, and syntax

Often, words are defined by more than just a dictionary definition. There are two methods of describing the meaning of words: denotative and connotative.

- **Denotative meaning**. This is the literal dictionary meanings of words. Although many words have multiple meanings and can function as different parts of speech, there is no hidden suggestion or symbolic meaning behind these definitions.

  - Example: A *rock* is a stone composed of some minerals; it can also refer to a genre of music.

  - Example: *Baggage* refers to personal belongings in a suitcase.

- **Connotative meaning**. This is the suggested meaning influenced by culture and/or personal experience. These implied meanings are figurative and subjective because of the emotions or associations attached to them by each individual reader or writer. An author often uses words with positive, negative, or neutral connotations to communicate tone and mood.

  - Example: *Rock* can refer to someone who is always there for you and who you can rely on, as in *she was my **rock** during the difficult time in my life*. This word has a positive connotation in this example.

  - Example: *Baggage* has a negative connotation as it can refer to past experiences that are considered a burden, as in *he's carrying a lot of **baggage** to this situation*.

Read the paragraph below and identify how the words *electric current* and *charging* are being used in the paragraph.

She felt as if her excitement was charging the air, sending an electric current throughout the atmosphere as she dashed through the monumental entryway of her new workplace. Those around her zoomed past her, only concerned with being prompt to their own jobs.

    A. Connotative to set the tone for excitement

    B. Denotative to understand the meaning of the words

    C. Simile to compare two things

    D. Hyperbole to exaggerate

Correct Answer: A

In the paragraph, the words *electric current* and *charging* are used to show an excited and heightened mood. The meaning of these words in the paragraph is connotative or implied. Simile and hyperbole are not used in the paragraph.

As discussed previously, morphology is the study of words, word structure, and the various forms of words. Think stems, roots, prefixes, and suffixes.

A teaching example of this is a teacher may notice that students are not able to break words down to determine meanings. She knows this skill is important for their comprehension of a variety of texts. The teacher can model a **structural analysis** of a word and then provide guided and independent practice opportunities to help build this essential skill. An example of structural analysis is illustrated below.

Example Structural Analysis

Word	Prefix	Root	Suffix	Definition
anti/path/y	against	feeling/emotion	abstract noun	hatred
a/path/y	not, without	feeling/emotion	abstract noun	indifference
em/path/y	into, cover with	feeling/emotion	abstract noun	to share another's emotions
sym/path/y	together, with	feeling/emotion	abstract noun	feelings of pity or sorrow

Understanding how word endings change the parts of speech or tense in words is another key component in morphology. For example, adding an *-s* to the end of *drive* makes the verb singular. Adding *-tion* to the verb *educate* makes the word an abstract noun.

Breaking down compound words is another way to help students understand meaning. Individually, the words have their own separate meanings; together, they form a whole new meaning.

Examples:

- *football*
- *moonlight*
- *sunflower*
- *crosswalk*
- *grandmother*
- *fireworks*

Quick Tip

If students are analyzing root words and their meaning, they are using ***etymology***.

Context clues

In reading and listening, a context clue is a form of information (such as a definition, synonym, antonym, or example) that appears near a word or phrase and offers direct or indirect suggestions about its meaning (Nordquist, 2020).

Synonym or restatement clues. These context clues restate the meaning of the word using a synonym. The sentence is essentially saying the same thing twice. For example, the sentence below contains a synonym or restatement clue.

Restatement clue

She was very <u>scrupulous</u> with her homework; she <u>meticulously completed every question.</u>

Vocab word

Synonym of the vocab word

Antonym or contrast clues. These context clues state the opposite of the word in question. For example, the sentence below contains an antonym or contrast clue.

Vocab word

Antonym or contrasting phrase

She thought of herself as <u>scrupulous</u>; <u>however, her work lacked detail, and she often missed her deadlines.</u>

Conjunctive adverb meaning the opposite

Inference clues. These context clues are subtle statements that drop hints to what the word in question is. For example, the sentence below contains

Inference clue

She was <u>scrupulous</u> in a way that <u>kept her up at night, obsessing over details in her emails.</u>

Vocab word

3. Print and digital reference materials

There are many resources and reference materials available to students. Therefore, students should be able to identify basic uses of these resources and tools.

Grammar/Style Guide	Dictionary	Thesaurus
• Grammar and usage rules • Conventional rules—capitalization, punctuation, spelling • Editing writing • Citation guidelines	• For a precise definition of a word • To confirm a working definition of a word from context • To find the part of speech of a word • To see the pronunciation/syllabication of a word • To hear the pronunciation of a word (digital version) • To check spelling • To find associated words • To find the etymology or origin of a word **Note:** There are specific etymological dictionaries, but most dictionaries will indicate where a word originated.	• To find synonyms, or words with similar meanings • To find antonyms, or words with opposite meanings

4. Dialect and diction across regions, cultural groups, and time periods

Language evolves and changes over time because language is influenced by different phenomena in the human experience. These include social, cultural, ethnic, religious, historical, regional, and gender influences.

Social influences

The fundamental use of language is to communicate with others. Therefore, language is a social construct, meaning language changes rapidly or slowly as communities use language. For this exam, you will be required to match words or phrases to their social influence.

Cultural and ethnic influences

Language is a cultural and ethnic tool people use to relate a community's values and ideals. Language is shaped and molded by communities over time. Embedded in our language are borrowed words, which are words adopted from other cultures. You might have an *armoire* in your bedroom, or you may be having a *fiesta* for your sister's birthday. These are examples of how culture and ethnicity influence language.

Religious influences

The spread of Christianity in early civilizations and the printing of the King James Bible introduced the masses to religious text, which filtered its way into everyday vernacular. Below are just a few examples of English words that have religious foundations.

- **Bonfire.** Originally, bone fires were used to burn the bodies of saints during the English Reformation.

- **Enthusiastic.** From the Greek *enthusiasmos*, "a god within." The word first meant "filled with God," as did *giddy*, from Anglo-Saxon *gydig*, "god-held man."

- **Excruciating.** The Latin word for "cross," *crux*, is embedded in the words *crucial* and *excruciating*.

Test Tip

You may be asked to identify literary text embedded with religious influences. *The Canterbury Tales* by Chaucer, *Paradise Lost* by Milton, and *Inferno* by Dante are all examples of important literary texts containing religious influence.

Historical influences

English is a Germanic language that has evolved through generations by crossing boundaries, and it continues to change over time. There are more non-native speakers of English than there are native English speakers. The development of the English language can be categorized into three primary historical periods:

- **Old English or Anglo-Saxon (450–1100 A.D.).** This form of English is barely recognizable to modern-day English speakers. During this time period, Anglo-Saxons and Jutes mixed their Germanic dialects. Later, Romans brought Latin influences to the language, followed by even more Latin infusion as a result of the spread of Christianity. Finally, the Vikings brought Norse influences. The epic poem Beowulf is an important work written in Old English; however, the version found in textbooks in today's classrooms is translated into Modern English with some short pieces shown in the original language.

- **Middle English (1100–1500).** The Duke of Normandy brought French-speaking nobles to run his new government after his successful invasion of England, thus bringing French influences into the language. After England and France split, many of those influences stuck, particularly words that denoted power such as crown, castle, court, parliament, army, mansion, and governor. Chaucer's *The Canterbury Tales* is an important work of this time.

- **Modern English (1500–present).** After William Caxton brought the printing press to England, Modern English became standardized. The language continued to change as the English Renaissance brought Greek and Latin words into the language. Then, the Industrial Revolution brought a slew of technical words as new machinery and technology emerged (camera, telegraph, engine, etc.) Finally, British Colonialism impacted the language as the British interacted with the inhabitants of the countries they conquered.

Think about it!

Etymology is the study of the origin of words and dynamic nature of their forms and meanings. In other words, where did the word come from and how has the word changed over time?

Regional influences

English usage or pronunciations can vary depending on the region in which they are used. These are called **dialects.** In American English, pronunciation varies by a person from New England versus a person from the South. Often, different words are used for the same item. For example, New Englanders call submarine sandwiches *grinders*. People from New Orleans call them *po' boys*. New Yorkers order *heroes*. Philadelphians ask for *hoagies*.

When speakers of different languages need to communicate with each other, they often create a simplified language called a **pidgin**. A pidgin is a form of communication with limited grammar and vocabulary between two groups that do not have a common language.

Gender influences

Language contains a substantial amount of gender bias. Think about words like *businessman, chairman, housewife.* As language changes, antiquated words are replaced with gender-neutral words like *businessperson, chairperson,* and the like.

Example question

His outfit was so *cool*. All of the other kids wanted to be him.

The use of the word *cool* in this sentence shows what influence on language?

   A. Social

   B. Historical

   C. Cultural

   D. Structural

Correct Answer: A

The word *cool* is a colloquialism or informal language embedded with social influences. The word *cool* is slang, and slang is a social aspect of language.

Test Tip

On the exam, you will most likely be asked to identify colloquialisms, denotative language, and connotative language.

- **Colloquialisms** are informal words and phrases. Another way to refer to colloquial language is *slang.* Colloquialisms are greatly affected by social influences.

- **Denotative meaning** is the dictionary meaning of a word. For example, the denotative meaning of *cool* is cold, or at a low temperature.

- **Connotative meaning** is the implied meaning. For example, the connotative meaning of the word *cool* is easy going, popular, or stylish.

5. Research-based approaches for supporting language acquisition and vocabulary development for diverse learners

The study of language

The study of language usually revolves around two main areas: phonology and morphology. You might encounter questions on the exam that require you to identify the difference between phonology and morphology.

Type	Description
Phonology	Phonology studies the **sound system** in a particular language and how the sound systems differ from language to language.
Morphology	Morphology studies the way words are put together to build **meaning**—it focuses on word structure and formation. Morphemes are the smallest units of meaning in words. Examples of morphemes are prefixes, suffixes, and root words. • **Root words**. The root word is the primary lexical unit of a word that carries the most meaning. The root word for *incredible* is *cred* or *believe*. • **Prefixes**. Additions to root words that help to form a new word with another meaning from that of the root word. Prefixes are at the beginning of a word. • **Suffixes**. Additions to root words that form a new word with another meaning from that of the root word. Suffixes are at the end of a word. They change the part of speech or verb tense (past tense, present tense) of a word. They also indicate whether the word is plural or singular.

Example question

A tenth-grade English class is working through difficult words by focusing on the smallest meanings in the word. For example, in the word *malevolent,* students discuss how *mal* means bad or evil so they can ascertain that the word carries a negative meaning. When they look up the word in the dictionary, the students see they are correct and that even though they don't know that word right away, they can figure out the meaning by using the structure of the word. This activity is focusing on which of the following?

A. Phonology

B. Morphology

C. Etymology

D. Dialect

Correct Answer: B

The students looked at the root and determined correctly that the word has a negative meaning because the root *mal* means evil. Using prefixes, suffixes, and roots to figure out the small meanings in words is morphology.

Emergent reading and word recognition skills

Because you will be teaching struggling readers and English learners, you must have a general understanding of the basic skills of word recognition.

Skill	Description	Example
Phonemic awareness	Phonemic awareness, a subset of phonological awareness, is understanding and manipulating the individual phonemes, or sounds, in words. Connect phonemic awareness to **sounds** only.	Having phonemic awareness allows a student to separate the sounds in the word *cat* into three distinct individual sounds: /k/, /æ/, and /t/. It also allows the student to know that when the /k/ sound is removed and /b/ sound replaces it, the sounds change to /b/ /a/ /t/.
Phonics	Phonics focuses on how the sounds connect to spelling (e.g., letter-sound correspondences). The learner is able to recognize letters and their corresponding sounds.	In the word *chain*, the consonant sound /ch/ is represented by two letters: c + h. The student has to **see** the word to make the c+h letter-sound connection.
Phonological awareness	Phonological awareness is the ability to use phonemic awareness and phonics to recognize and read words.	Having phonological awareness means being able to use sounds, spelling, and syllables to identify words.

Example Problem

Ms. Ruiz is working with English language learners (ELLs) in a small group. She is helping her students understand that *-tion* in words makes a **shun** sound. They are working on which of the following?

A. Phonological awareness

B. Phonics

C. Phonemic awareness

D. Prefixes

Correct Answer: B

Because they are working on how the spelling of a word corresponds with a sound, the students are working on phonics. You have to see the word or letters to use phonics.

Think of word recognition as an umbrella. Phonological awareness is the over-arching skill that encompasses phonemic awareness (sounds only). To have phonological awareness, you first must have phonemic awareness.

Vocabulary instruction

Effective vocabulary instruction will help students become better readers, writers, and critical thinkers. However, effective vocabulary instruction should involve using words in context and across disciplines. Asking students to memorize a list of 10 vocabulary words per week is not effective vocabulary instruction. Using a dictionary to look up words and record definitions is not effective either. A more effective way is to use the vocabulary words in context.

Context clues are words or phrases that come before or after the unknown vocabulary word and help explain its meaning. A dictionary is a valuable tool, but it should not be the only thing teachers use for vocabulary instruction.

Vocabulary tiers

There are three tiers of vocabulary: basic, high frequency, and context-specific. The frequency of use, complexity, and meaning determine the tier of a vocabulary word.

- **Tier I words (basic)**. These are commonly used words with standard definitions. These are words used in everyday American English.

- **Tier II words (high frequency)**. These words show up frequently in a variety of texts, but they are more complex than tier I words. Think about the eighth-grade tier II words *perspective, depict, evidence,* and *contrast*. These words can show up across the curriculum, particularly in task directions.

- **Tier III words (domain-specific)**. These are words students are not familiar with because they do not cross the curriculum and must be explicitly and systematically taught by the content area teacher. For example, students in a biology class must know the meaning of *nucleotide*, but knowing that word will not help them in math, social studies, or English.

Quick Tip

Effective vocabulary instruction goes beyond memorizing definitions; it provides multiple exposures and opportunities for usage in oral and written language. It also employs a variety of strategies, such as **context clues**, word part analysis, and word relationships

Vocabulary Tiers

Tier I Words	Tier II Words	Tier III Words
• Common words • Used in everyday speech • Learned in early years	• Academic language • Not specific to a particular discipline • Frequently encountered in written text (fiction and informational) • Subtle or precise ways to communicate a thought	• Technical language • Specific to a particular discipline • Not familiar to most students • Necessary to understand a topic • Far more common in informational texts

Scenario

In her English III class, Ms. Perry has identified a list of words from a particular text that are essential for her students' understanding. Instead of giving these words to her students to look up in a dictionary, define, and use in a sentence, she has students help her create an interactive word wall to use during the unit. She also finds shorter texts that include the target words. Ms. Perry models using context clues, asks students to come up with a working definition, and provides guided and independent practice opportunities. For one of the words that lends itself to word part analysis, she models breaking down the word by roots, prefixes, and suffixes, then has her students practice with the remainder of the words in cooperative centers. Through multiple and varied exposures, her students will be able to comprehend the words permanently and be able to use them accurately in speech and writing.

Assessing language skills

Language skills can be assessed in multiple ways. Multiple choice tests are usually not the best way to see if students understand the complexities of these skills. Teachers need to see if their students can (1) identify language and grammar elements in other people's writing and (2) use language elements in their own writing. Students learn about grammar, vocabulary, and literary tools through reading and writing tasks. The teacher can informally assess student's language skills by:

- Using a writing rubric (even for short answers) that focuses on language skills. For example, if sentence variation is lacking in essays, the teacher can choose to grade only for sentence variation.

- Using bell ringers or exit tickets that quickly assess one language skill. For example, have students identify and interpret an author's use of one figurative language device after reading a passage.

- Having students use language in context. For example, construct a short speech using the language skills assessed in class.

Test Tip

On the exam, you might see the practice of using exit tickets associated with formative assessment. Formative assessments are ongoing informal checks teachers use to make instructional decisions. Exit tickets are an effective way to measure student understanding.

Assessing stages of cognitive development

It is helpful to understand Piaget's stages of cognitive development when teaching students English language arts concepts. Jean Piaget was an education researcher who asserted students pass through 4 distinct stages of cognitive development. Middle and high schoolers are usually at the concrete operational and formal operational stages.

Piaget's 4 Stages of Cognitive Development

Stage	Age	Description
Sensorimotor	0–2 years	Children at this stage figure out the world through sensory and motor experiences. Object permanence and separation anxiety are hallmarks of this stage.
Pre-operational	2–6 years	Children at this stage identify and use symbols for objects but do not have the ability to apply logical reasoning. They know how to play and are egocentric.
Concrete operational	7–12 years	Logical reasoning about concrete objects kicks in during this stage. Conservation, reversibility, serial ordering, and understanding cause and effect relationships are hallmarks of this stage, but thinking is still limited to the concrete.
Formal operational	12 years–adult	Abstract thinking, such as logic, deductive reasoning, comparison, and classification, is demonstrated by the individual in this stage.

Bloom's Taxonomy (Bloom, Englehart, Furst, Hill, & Krathwohl, 1956). This is a hierarchical model used to classify educational learning objectives into levels of complexity and specificity. The skills become more complex as you move higher on the pyramid. When answering questions regarding critical thinking, think about Bloom's Taxonomy.

Apply

Create

Analyze

Evaluate

Compare & Contrast

Categorize

Understand & Identify

Remember & Memorize

Note: *This is a modified Bloom's Taxonomy to show more skills than the original taxonomy.*

Teaching language skills

Pedagogy is the theory and practice of teaching. Below are some instructional methods that teachers should be familiar with.

- **Integrated curriculum.** This is all about interconnectedness and interrelationships between and among content areas (all about making connections). For example, the English teacher plans a lesson around what students are learning in social science class. Integrated curriculum may also be referred to as cross-curricular, interdisciplinary, and multidisciplinary curriculum. Activities should be authentic and related to real life. Students are seen as active learners who research, interpret, and process learning to others and themselves.

- **Differentiated instruction.** This is a framework for effective teaching that addresses learners' various needs (e.g., various abilities, strengths/weaknesses, and readiness). For example, the teacher makes sure the task suits the students' learning styles, is careful when grouping students, and uses authentic lessons and problem-based activities (Weselby, 2014).

  - **Differentiated content.** This is when teachers have a variety of subjects based on students' interests or readiness. For example, based on leveled groups, students analyze poems at varying difficulty levels.

  - **Differentiated process.** This is when a teacher modifies instruction to meet the various needs of the students in the class. This is often done using flexible groups. For example, after a short, whole-group lesson on metaphors, students split into small groups to analyze concepts.

  - **Differentiated product.** This is when the teacher allows students to choose how they show mastery of a concept or skill. For example, the teacher allows students to write a persuasive essay, design a brochure, record a podcast, or build a presentation to show mastery of the standard. This taps into students' learning preferences.

Test Tip

On the exam, you might see questions about **differentiation** and **scaffolding**. These are on the good words list. Scaffolding is providing support to students to help them achieve the standard. In this technique, teachers do NOT make the lesson easier or change expectations. Instead, teachers employ strategies to support students in their learning.

Teaching grammar, usage, and punctuation

The desired instructional outcome is not that students are successful in memorizing rules; the desired outcome is that students gain the ability to transfer and use language skills in their writing. The most effective way to teach these skills is within the framework of student writing. It bears repeating, using drills and worksheets are usually not the correct answers on the test.

What would this look like in the classroom?

- **If it is a whole-class issue:**
    - Use writing samples with whole-group instruction. Then, employ a writing workshop (students write best when they write frequently, for extended periods of time, on topics of their own choosing) to have students work on the skill using a piece of their own writing. The teacher offers support in a teacher-led center.

- **If it is a different issue for different students:**
    - Split the students into differentiated groups to workshop their writing in a way that is specific to their needs. The teacher offers support in a teacher-led center.

- **If it is an individual student issue:**
    - Pull students for individual conferencing while the class works in small groups on a targeted skill (after a short, directly instructed mini-lesson).

Teaching vocabulary (including connotative/denotative meanings)

There are many engaging ways to teach vocabulary; however, vocabulary instruction should be meaningful and long-lasting for students. The most effective way to teach vocabulary is by asking students to use semantic (context) clues to develop a working definition.

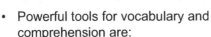

Quick Tip

Use glossaries and digital or print dictionaries only when a precise denotative meaning is necessary or to confirm working definitions.

- Powerful tools for vocabulary and comprehension are:
    - Word walls
    - Close readings
    - Context clues
    - Word part analysis (prefix-root-suffix)

Second language acquisition – English language learners

English teachers have to prepare for students in the class who are learning English as a second language. First language (L1) acquisition refers to the way children learn their native language. Second language (L2) acquisition refers to the learning of another language or languages other than the native language. Typically, language acquisition is associated with English language learners (ELLs). Below are the stages an ELL goes through during second language acquisition (Krashen & Terrell, 1983).

Stage	Description
1 **Pre-production**	This is commonly known as the silent period. Learners have receptive vocabulary (listening), but they are not speaking yet. In this stage, repetition is key. The learner watches and listens in an attempt to absorb the language.
2 **Early production**	The learner starts to use some words but has not yet mastered forming sentences. Stage 2 may last up to six months. Students will develop more receptive and active vocabulary. Using memorization, chunking, and pictures (just as in first language acquisition) is helpful in this stage.
3 **Speech emergence**	The learner uses short phrases, simple sentences, and simple questions that may or may not be correct. He or she begins to understand simple phrases in this stage. Vocabulary is more developed.
4 **Intermediate fluency**	The learner has a much better grasp on the language as he or she begins to comprehend information taught in the second language and speaks in longer, complex sentences. Students have an active vocabulary and begin using questioning techniques to clarify meaning. It is in this stage that learners begin to think in their second language.
5 **Advanced fluency**	The learner speaks and understands the new language with little to no support. This is when students demonstrate cognitive language proficiency to go beyond the basics and think/respond critically in the acquired language. It can take students 4-10 years to achieve academic proficiency in a second language. Occasional support is still needed.

Chart adapted from Haynes (2005)

In order to meet the specific needs of English speakers of other languages (ESOL) and ELLs, teachers can differentiate instruction. Teachers must pay attention to a student's L1 to advance the student's L2. Therefore, teachers should embrace students speaking their first language. Research shows that mastery in L1 is essential in mastering L2 (Larsen-Freeman & Long, 1991).

Test Tip

The most common modification for ELLs in English instruction is to use pictures and graphics to support ELLs' understanding of meaning.

World-class Instructional Design and Assessment

World-class Instructional Design and Assessment (WIDA) is an organization that creates standards and assessments to help with the instruction of ELLs. WIDA supports students, families, educators, and administrators with research-based tools and resources. WIDA standards align for students from kindergarten through grade 12. The WIDA framework includes five components that are interactive and interdependent. These components exemplify the WIDA vision for academic language development (WIDA, 2012).

Quick Tip

We recommend that you visit the WIDA website for more information on this topic. Be sure to review the language development standards at wida.wisc.edu.

Common grammatical errors made by English language learners

Grammar usage by ELLs is different than that of native speakers. Some learners make minor errors, which are easily corrected, while others make errors that impede comprehension. Below are some common errors that ELLs make (Folse, 2009). ELA teachers should be able to explain why an error is incorrect.

- **Prepositions**
    - Example: She was born on 1956.
    - Correction: She was born in 1956.
- **Present perfect**
    - Example: I have been to Florida in 2015.
    - Correction: I have been to Florida.
    - Correction: I was in Florida in 2015.
- **Phrasal verbs**
    - Example: There is no concert because the singer called off it.
    - Correction: There is no concert because the singer called it off.
- **Count and noncount nouns**
    - Example: How many homeworks do we have?
    - Correction: How much homework do we have?
- **Gerunds and infinitives**
    - Example: I avoid to give money to my kids.
    - Correction: I avoid giving money to my kids.
- **Modals**
    - Example: I must to study tonight.
    - Correction: I must study tonight.
- **Passive voice**
    - Example: I was sleeping when the party was happened.
    - Correction: I was sleeping when the party happened.

English language learner teaching strategies

Pedagogy is the act of teaching. When instructing students who are ELLs, teachers must keep pedagogy in mind and accommodate to help students with language acquisition. There are many ways to scaffold or support instruction for English learners. The following table provides some strategies and suggestions that teachers can implement to help their ELLs.

Strategy	Explanation
Provide visual aids	• Use pictures, hands on materials, and other visual tools. • When teaching vocabulary, present the word and a picture to resemble the concept that is being taught. • Use the whiteboard to write directions for class procedures instead of verbalizing them.
Foster cooperative learning	• Allow students to work collaboratively in groups. For example, when analyzing meaning in text, students engage in literature circles—small groups engaging in text analysis.
Honor the "silent period"	• The "silent period" is part of the learning process. • Allowing the student to stay quiet, observe, and learn will benefit the student's ability to continually learn in the classroom.
Allow use of native language	• Allowing students to continue to use their native language until they build proficiency in their second language is a way to scaffold instruction. • Teachers should provide ELLs with adapted text and offer choice in text selection.
Teach thematically	• This type of instruction focuses on a specific theme; it is teaching multiple content areas and skills using the same theme. • It is important that each unit integrates reading, writing, speaking, and listening skills. • Thematic units can help learners draw connections from the real world, and thematic instruction can promote learners' linguistic and cognitive development.
Provide context	• This is especially important for grammar and vocabulary instruction.

(Gonzalez, 2014)

Example Questions and Answer Explanations

1. A tenth-grade teacher wants to reinforce how to use complex sentences in compositional writing. Which of the following would be most effective in reinforcing these skills so students can apply them to increase sentence variety in their writing?

   A. Diagram complex sentences and evaluate how dependent and independent clauses contribute to sentence variety.

   B. Look up complex words in the dictionary and use them appropriately to make the writing more complex and varied.

   C. Have students complete grammar worksheets and practice sentence skills so the skills become automatic.

   D. Have students work in cooperative groups to identify complex sentences in the text.

2. Ms. Ruiz's class is reading *The Immortal Life of Henrietta Lacks*, a non-fiction book about a woman who unknowingly donated her cancer cells to Johns Hopkins Research Hospital in 1951. The book contains biology vocabulary that may be confusing to students. What can Ms. Ruiz do to support students?

   A. Work on tier I words

   B. Work on tier II words

   C. Work on tier III words

   D. Work on tier IV words

3. Mr. Jackson, a tenth-grade English teacher, has several students who are ELLs in class. The students have strong reading aloud skills and conversational skills. However, they struggle with critical meaning of complex text. Mr. Jackson knows this is because the students' first language is not English. What would be the most effective approach Mr. Jackson can take with these students?

   A. Request the students be admitted to an ESOL class.

   B. Scaffold instruction when the students need help.

   C. Group all the ELLs together and work on word drills.

   D. Request a paraprofessional for class to help translate for students.

4. Ms. Jones is introducing a new grammar concept for students to use in their writing. Which of the following would be most effective for explicit instruction for this lesson?

   A. Whole-group lesson where the teacher projects sentences on the whiteboard and models how to use proper grammar

   B. Cooperative learning workshops where students use the new grammar concepts and check each other's work

   C. Repetitive at-home practice where students work with their parents and come back to class and share what they learned

   D. Individually work on grammar drills where students complete a worksheet and then go over it with a partner

5. The student writes the following sentence. Identify the error the student used.

   Even though the students' went to the party, they told their parents they were at the library.

   A. Separating independent and dependent clauses with a comma

   B. Maintaining subject-verb agreement

   C. Maintaining pronoun-antecedent agreement

   D. Understanding possessive nouns

6. A teacher is working with students on vocabulary for an upcoming novel about the Civil War. What would be the most effective way to reinforce complex historical vocabulary?

   A. Use an interactive word wall.

   B. Look up words in a dictionary.

   C. Read through the text and stop at confusing words.

   D. Have students define words for homework before reading.

7. Mr. Habakern is a ninth-grade English teacher who is working with a small group of ELLs who are in the developing stage of English language acquisition. Which of the following would be most effective in differentiating instruction for these students?

   A. Have each student read aloud and correct them when they mispronounce words or phrases.

   B. Time students when they read and calculate correct words read per minute.

   C. Require students to use English only to help them acquire English more quickly.

   D. Use pictures to represent overall themes in the book and relate the text to the pictures.

8. A teacher is working with several 8th grade students who are English language learners (ELLs). The teacher is focusing on prefixes, suffixes, and root words to help these students identify meaning. Which of the following aspects of language is the teacher working on?

   A. Phonemic awareness

   B. Phonics

   C. Morphology

   D. Syntax

9. A teacher is working with students on using antonyms as context clues to figure out difficult words in text. She shows students sentences with a new vocabulary word underlined. Which of the following would be an appropriate example of using antonyms to figure out words?

   A. Mainstream thinking lacks the unconventional quirkiness necessary for innovation.

   B. The apathetic teenager was careless about her homework or anything else.

   C. Animal cells use cellular respiration, the process animal cells go through to generate ATP from food.

   D. She was the matriarch, the female leader of the family.

10. Which of the following would be most effective in helping ELLs who are just learning English with their speaking skills?

A. Have ELLs give formal oral presentations in front of the class.

B. Have ELLs work in small groups to use English to roleplay different real-world scenarios.

C. Have students draw pictures of different speaking scenarios.

D. Have a fluent speaker of English tutor ELLs on speaking skills.

Number	Answer	Explanation
1.	A	Answer choice A is the only answer choice where students are evaluating sentence structure and how it can be used to increase sentence variety. This is the most effective approach.
2.	C	**Tier I words** – the, and, she, go, walk **Tier II words** – inspiration, indecisive, unconscious **Tier III words** – mitochondria, deoxyribose nucleic acid, malignant, benign **Tier IV words** – there are no tier IV words.
3.	B	Scaffolding instruction is on the good words and practices list for this exam. Requesting students be put in an ESOL program or asking a paraprofessional to translate is ineffective. These students are fluent and need support. Grouping all English language learners (ELLs) together for word drills is least effective in this situation.
4.	A	This is a new concept, and the question asks specifically for an explicit instruction activity. Therefore, answer choice A is best because a whole-group activity where the teacher models the lesson is explicit instruction. This is typically the way teachers should introduce new concepts. Later, the students can move into cooperative workshop groups. Homework, drills, and worksheets are on the bad words list, so avoid those answer choices on the exam.
5.	D	The student incorrectly uses the apostrophe in the word *students,* indicating this student needs support in possessive nouns.
6.	A	An interactive word wall is a display of words on a classroom wall. The words can be taken on and off the wall (interactive). In this example, the wall would have words pertaining to the Civil War. The teacher might say, "Jose, go to the wall and choose two words that relate to President Lincoln." Jose then pics words like *The Emancipation Proclamation* and *The Gettysburg Address*. Then, the teacher has him explain why he chose those words. Then, Jose explains the connection between the words and President Lincoln. This is the most effective practice out of the activities listed.
7.	D	Students in the developing stage of language acquisition benefit from visual and graphic support when reading. Correcting students as they read aloud is bad practice, so avoid answer choice A. Always wait until there is a break in reading to scaffold for students when needed. Calculating words per minute (wpm) is not effective in this situation, eliminating answer choice B. Finally, research shows that English-only practices are less effective than bilingual approaches. Always avoid English-only practices on this exam and in your own classroom. Supporting the heritage or home language while increasing English exposure and use is most effective, according to research.

Number	Answer	Explanation
8.	C	Morphology is the basis of language and has to do with the way words are put together to build meaning—it focuses on word structure and formation. **Morphemes** are the smallest units of meaning in words. Examples of morphemes are prefixes and suffixes. **Phonemic Awareness** – Sounds **Phonics** – Spelling **Syntax** – Grammar
9.	A	Answer choice A uses an antonym for *mainstream*—unconventional. Answer choice B uses a synonym for *apathetic*—careless. Answer choice C uses a definition for *cellular respiration*—the process animal cells go through to generate ATP. Answer choice D uses a restatement/definition for *matriarch*—the female leader of the family.
10.	B	Having students work in small groups is less intimidating than giving a speech to the entire class. Answer B also outlines a real-world activity, which is always the best approach when learning a new language.

 # Writing, Speaking, and Listening

III. Writing, Speaking, and Listening

1. Various modes of writing

2. Task, purpose, and audience awareness

3. Characteristics of clear and coherent writing

4. Effective and ethical research practices: credibility of multiple print and digital sources, gathering relevant information, and citing sources accurately

5. Characteristics of effective speech and presentation

6. Effective use of digital media to support and enhance communication

7. Research-based approaches to teaching writing

8. Assessing reading, writing, speaking, and listening

9. Effective oral communication in a variety of settings

10. Awareness of various perspectives, cultures, and backgrounds when reading, writing, listening, and speaking

1. Various modes of writing

English teachers play a pivotal role in helping students communicate effectively in writing and helping students meet writing standards. In middle and high school, students must use various forms of writing to convey ideas. For example, students must write differently in science class than they do in social studies. Similarly, students must write creatively in English class and informatively in economics class.

Before beginning a writing task, writers should always consider two things:

1. **Audience** – who the writing is intended for

2. **Purpose** – what the writer is trying to accomplish

For example, a student will write differently to a U.S. senator than she would to her own grandmother. A student will also write differently for a research report than he would a sales brochure. On the exam, you will be required to show your understanding of each form of writing and how they can be applied in classroom scenarios.

Test Tip

On the exam, look for answers that allude to helping students understand the audience for and purpose of the writing. These two elements show up frequently.

There are five main forms of writing: descriptive, expository, narrative, persuasive, and argumentative. Each form has a specific purpose and specific characteristics.

Forms of Writing

Form of Writing	Description	Narrative
Descriptive	This type of writing employs imagery to describe. Metaphors and symbols are often used in descriptive writing.	First person Third person
Expository	This type of writing aims to inform the reader and is objective and free of bias. Expository writing is most commonly found in textbooks.	Third person
Narrative	This type of writing tells a story and often uses description. However, it differs from descriptive writing in that it includes action and is told from first-person point of view. Typically, this type of writing has a plot, rising action, climax, characters, and setting.	First person
Persuasive	This type of writing aims to convince the reader to adopt the author's opinion. In persuasive writing, the author chooses one side of the issue, takes a position, and maintains that position throughout the essay. The language the author uses in persuasive writing is often emotional.	First person Third person
Argumentative	This type of writing argues a point but presents multiple sides or perspectives of an issue. The goal is to get the reader to acknowledge that the arguments are valid and worthy of consideration.	First Person Third Person

2. Task, purpose, and audience awareness

Recall that students must consider the purpose and audience for the writing. For example, if a student is writing a thank you note to her grandmother for a gift, informal language and a personal, friendly tone is appropriate. However, if this same student is writing a thank you note to a prospective employer for an interview opportunity, the format, language, and tone must be formal and professional.

- **Purpose.** The purpose is the reason for communicating with someone. Generally, authors write to express an idea or opinion, provide information, provide an explanation, explore a topic, or argue a point (National Council for Teachers of English, 2006).

- **Audience.** The audience is the person or people for whom the communication is intended. As a writer, it is essential to understand the target audience. Otherwise, the purpose will not be met. Writers should consider the age, gender, education, socioeconomic status, culture, etc. when identifying their audience. Once they have pinpointed the dynamics of the audience, they can make sure to use language and information that will interest and inform or influence the readers (National Council for Teachers of English, 2006).

English language arts standards for text types and purposes

The Common Core State Standards (CCSS) for English language arts (ELA) grades 9-10 lay out the skills for writing for different purposes. Understanding these standards is helpful in planning purposeful lessons in writing. The following are the writing standards for argumentative, expository, and narrative writing.

Text types and purposes:

CCSS.ELA-LITERACY.W.9-10.1

Write arguments to support claims in an analysis of substantive topics or texts, using valid reasoning and relevant and sufficient evidence.

CCSS.ELA-LITERACY.W.9-10.2

Write informative/explanatory texts to examine and convey complex ideas, concepts, and information clearly and accurately through the effective selection, organization, and analysis of content.

CCSS.ELA-LITERACY.W.9-10.3

Write narratives to develop real or imagined experiences or events using effective technique, well-chosen details, and well-structured event sequences.

Quick Tip

Evidence is a key component in all English language arts writing standards. Students MUST support their claims in writing by citing evidence from the text. That can be a quick reference or a formal citation. Either way, students must use evidence from the text or other sources to validate their arguments.

Timed Writing

Throughout their academic career, students will encounter timed writing assessments. The focus of a timed writing piece is usually organization, clarity, and cohesiveness. Errors in grammar and spelling are usually not the focus of a timed writing task—as long as the errors are minor and do not negatively impact the meaning or understanding of the piece. The following are important elements of the timed writing task.

- **Plan effectively**. With limited time, students must map their plan of action quickly. They must:
  - Evaluate the prompt.
  - Identify the writing task.
  - Map the essay.

- **Develop a strong thesis.** Students must set the purpose for writing with a clear thesis statement. Students must use a variety of techniques for this.
  - Directly address the task of the prompt in the thesis.
  - Clearly state the purpose of writing.

- **Organize the essay**. It is often helpful for students to have a formula for organizing their essays. For example, an expository essay can be four paragraphs—one introduction paragraph, two details paragraphs, and one concluding paragraph. Structure will vary depending on the purpose of the essay.
  - Start with the details first.
  - Content should be organized in paragraphs by topic or idea.

- **Revise and edit**. Because revisions are so important, students must budget time for a quick but thorough revision process.
  - Revise - Check for gaps in organization.
  - Edit - Identify and correct spelling and grammar issues.

A teacher is working with students on the following standard:

CCSS.ELA-LITERACY.W.9-10.2

Write informative/explanatory texts to examine and convey complex ideas, concepts, and information clearly and accurately through the effective selection, organization, and analysis of content.

Which of the following classroom activities would be most effective in building the skills outlined in the standard?

A. Have students write letters to their parents inviting them to parent night and explaining all the activities happening during parent night.

B. Have students work in writing workshops to explore and brainstorm topics and discuss ideas for their upcoming research paper.

C. Give students 3 different writing prompts and have students practice mapping and structuring their essays quickly and efficiently based on the prompts.

D. Have students exchange papers to conduct peer reviews to edit mistakes or inaccuracies and assign a grade to the papers.

Correct Answer: C

The writing standard in the question requires students to write informational text in an organized manner. Answer choice C is the only answer choice where students are focused on organization. Answer choice A outlines a narrative piece of writing. Answer choice B is about brainstorming, not organizing informational text. Answer choice D is at the final stage of writing. This question is asking you to help students write informatively using organization and analysis of content.

3. Characteristics of clear and coherent writing

Effective English teachers focus ample instructional time on evidence-based writing. The national and state English language arts (ELA) standards outline students' abilities to write arguments to support claims ***using valid reasoning and relevant and sufficient evidence*** (Common Core State Standards, 2019). According to the ELA standards below, students should be able to do the following:

CCSS.ELA-LITERACY.W.9-10.4

Produce clear and coherent writing in which the development, organization, and style are appropriate to task, purpose, and audience.

CCSS.ELA-LITERACY.W.9-10.5

Develop and strengthen writing as needed by planning, revising, editing, rewriting, or trying a new approach, focusing on addressing what is most significant for a specific purpose and audience.

CCSS.ELA-LITERACY.W.9-10.6

Use technology, including the Internet, to produce, publish, and update individual or shared writing products, taking advantage of technology's capacity to link to other information and to display information flexibly and dynamically.

Test Tip

The language used in the ELA standards is often the same language you'll see in the correct answer choices on the exam. Never underestimate the importance of reading the standards. The exams are designed to assess your understanding of the state and national standards. Paying attention to what is in the standards will not only help you on the test, but it will help you focus your instruction in the classroom.

III. WRITING, SPEAKING, AND LISTENING

Students use different forms of writing for different purposes. In addition to using different forms of writing, effective English teachers show students how to use different text structures to focus writing on purpose and task.

Text Structure	Definition	Key Words and Phrases
Cause and effect	This structure is used when the author wants to show why something happened.	therefore, because, as a result, leading to, consequently, for this reason, the effect of
Compare/contrast	This structure is used to show the similarities and differences of two or more things.	as well as, either...or, instead of, both, on the other hand, as opposed to, similarly, in contrast
Description	The author describes features or characteristics of a topic by using vivid imagery.	to illustrate, for instance, the characteristics of, an example, such as
Problem/solution	This structure is used when an author wants to explore an issue and address possible solutions.	to solve this, the issue at hand, one reason for this problem, a possible solution
Sequence/ chronology	This structure is used to describe events in order, often by time, year, or event.	first, second, next, then, before, after, finally

Writing an essay or story can take several days or even weeks to complete. It is imperative that students understand that in real-world situations, writing requires students to revise and improve their original work until they have something worthy of publishing. These steps are not linear; a writer may revise and restructure the essay several times before publishing. It is important that English teachers guide students through the steps in the writing process as learning opportunities.

In other words, these steps are formative in nature because students are using feedback to revise and improve their writing.

- **Prewriting.** This is often referred to as planning. It includes the collection and organization of ideas that occur before writing. Some common prewriting strategies include:

  - Brainstorming and listing
  - Researching
  - Outlining
  - Clustering and mind mapping
  - Discussing

- **Drafting.** The first iteration of a piece of writing. This is where the author starts to put ideas down on paper and develop a text structure. Drafting is not the final product.

Quick Tip

Students can use the prewriting strategy **SOAPStone**, which is an acronym to remember what students should consider before they write.

Subject

Occasion

Audience

Purpose

Speaker

Tone

- **Peer review.** During this part of the writing process, students workshop each other's draft essays. Students read for content and understanding and provide suggestions. This is an important step in establishing an organized, cohesive essay.

- **Revising.** During this part of the writing process, students improve their rough drafts by adding, deleting, rewording, and arranging words and phrases. This is where students will make sure their tone is appropriate for the purpose and intended audience. Although people often lump revising and editing together, they are not the same. In the revision stage, the writers are looking at how their paragraphs work into the essay as a whole. Some common revising techniques include:

    - Peer review

    - Teacher conferencing

    - Writing workshops

- **Editing.** At this stage, the writers are examining their sentences for grammar, spelling, and mechanics. Students proofread their essays and fix punctuation and spelling errors.

- **Publishing.** At this stage, students have put the work into the world for people to read. Publishing can include mailing a letter to the editor, pressing send on an email, publishing a formal essay, or displaying a poster in the library.

Example question

A teacher is having students conduct a peer review. She asks students to revise each other's papers. What are the students focusing on?

    A. Point of view

    B. Use of descriptive language

    C. Grammar and punctuation

    D. Ideas and organization

Correct Answer: D

Revision is the process of reorganizing writing based on ideas and logical sequence. Reviewing for grammar and punctuation is editing. Answers choices A and B are not applicable to this scenario.

Think about it!

While often used interchangeably, revising and editing are very different. Revising is restructuring your writing based on organization and understanding. Editing is reading line by line correcting grammar and spelling. Be sure to remember this difference when taking the exam.

RAFT Strategy

RAFT is an effective writing strategy to help students practice writing for different audiences and occasions. RAFT stands for (R) role of the writer, (A) audience, (F) format, and (T) topic. This strategy helps students learn how to communicate their ideas effectively. It also helps them to consider the purpose for writing, the audience, and the topic. Below are sample questions students can consider when preparing to write:

Role: What is your role?

Audience: Who is your audience?

Format: What format are you going to use to write?

Topic: What's the topic?

Classroom scenario

The entire class is reading *The Great Gatsby* by F. Scott Fitzgerald. They are using the RAFT strategy to explore different topics and characters in the text and write an essay from those perspectives. The teacher displays four different options students can use to write their essays.

Raft Example – *The Great Gatsby*

R	A	F	T
Jay Gatsby	Students at Oxford	Speech	Why it's better to be rich rather than poor.
Nick Carraway	Nick Carraway	Diary Entry	Jay Gatsby's secrets.
Daisy Buchanan	Police	Police Report	What happened to Myrtle Wilson?
Myrtle Wilson	Friends and family	Obituary	Why money is not always the most important thing.

4. **Effective and ethical research practices: credibility of multiple print and digital sources, gathering relevant information, and citing sources accurately**

It is imperative for students to understand that not all sources of information, online or in print, are reputable. Students need to critically evaluate sources to ensure that the information is credible. Here are some guidelines:

- **Academic journals**. The most credible sources of objective, relevant, and reliable information are peer-reviewed, academic journals that contain scholarly articles and educational research and dissertations.

   – Check for a bibliography. This is a sign that the source is credible.

- **Internet**. Online sources ending in *.gov* and *.edu* are usually reliable, government-sponsored sites. However, sometimes scammers purchase domains with *.gov* and .edu, so make sure students thoroughly check for signs of authenticity.

- **Organizations**. URLs ending in *.org* are generally non-profit organizations that can provide useful information but can also be filled with bias.

Students need to look at all sites with healthy skepticism to identify if the information presented is objective or if there is a hidden or obvious agenda.

Although writing a research paper is an essential academic skill, it can be a rigorous process. Teachers who assign research papers must set students up for success by guiding them through this long and important process.

Quick Tip

When collecting reference materials or information for a writing project, help students locate and examine the bibliography so students can decipher reliable information from unreliable information.

Steps in the research process

The following six steps outline the strategy for writing a research paper (North Hennepin Community College, n.d.)

1. Identify the topic.
2. Search for information.
3. Locate source materials.
4. Evaluate sources for reliability and validity.
5. Take notes.
6. Produce the product (research paper, presentation, etc.)

Evaluating sources

Students must be taught how to evaluate source information for relevancy, validity, and reliability, but this is especially important with Internet sources. In addition, the collected information must be relevant to the topic of inquiry.

- **Peer-reviewed journals/articles.** These sources are found on a database and can be considered credible. These are appropriate to use when students need very specific research information on a topic; however, they are not very helpful for general background information. Examples of databases where scholarly journals are stored are ProQuest, SAGE, and EBSCOhost. Examples of journals within these databases are The Social Science Journal, The American Journal of Psychology, The New England Journal of Medicine, etc.

- **Websites.** Websites are effective for gathering general information. Students can use websites to gather background information, evaluate different perspectives on a topic, and obtain current news events. Things like ads and heavy political or controversial opinion statements are red flags that the site is biased and unreliable.

- **Print sources (books, newspapers, magazines).** Books can be an appropriate place to start for historical information or context. Magazines and newspapers will be useful for current events in an easy-to-understand format.

Synthesizing

Synthesizing includes making connections, combining important topics, and developing a summary. Keep in mind:

- Synthesizing reports information from multiple sources.
- Synthesizing interprets the source information to help the reader gain a deeper understanding.

Paraphrasing

Paraphrasing is describing something in your own words. It is important that when students use information from other people's research or work, students must accurately cite that information. Even if students paraphrase, they still borrowed the idea from another writer. Common knowledge, such as well-known and accepted dates and facts, does not need to be referenced.

Avoiding plagiarism

It is important to teach students how to cite source material. Typically, **MLA** (Modern Language Association) is used for English, literature, and humanities, and **APA** (American Psychological Association) is used for science, social science, and technical courses. To assist students across content areas, teaching them when and how to use the appropriate format is key. Just like writing style, different citation methods are appropriate for different audiences and tasks. It is helpful to know the general guidelines of in-text citations and how the works cited/references pages are formatted. Always consult the latest edition of the *MLA Handbook* and the *Publication Manual of the American Psychological Association* to ensure citations are accurate.

Test Tip

A multiple-choice test is NOT an effective way to assess students' citation (MLA or APA) skills. The best way to assess these skills is to apply these skills. For example, have students complete a research project or paper with citations. These do not always have to be huge, drawn-out assignments. Mini research projects work just as well. Students should be taught to take detailed notes and quote any direct words or phrases from the text in order to avoid *accidental plagiarism.*

Citing and referencing sources

Citations should occur within the body of the document. These are called in-text citations or parenthetical citations.

Citations should also be included on a works cited page (MLA) or references page (APA) at the end of the document.

Note: Citations should always occur in the document (in-text) and at the end of the document in a list. They should be in both places.

Quick Tip

The main thing to look for when determining whether the citation is MLA or APA is where the date is located in the citation.

- **APA.** Text contains a bibliography or reference page. In-text citations have the last name of the author and date.

- **MLA.** Text contains a works cited page. In-text citations have last name of the author and page number.

Sample APA and MLA Citations

Source	Format	Bibliography/Works Cited	In-Text Citation
Book	APA	Gleick, James. Chaos: Making a New Science. Penguin, 1987.	(Tolstoy, 1969)
	MLA	Tolstoy, L. (1869). War and peace. Moscow: Viking.	(Sullivan 120)
Journal article	APA	Wegener, D. T., & Petty, R. E. (1994). Mood management across affective states: The hedonic contingency hypothesis. Journal of Personality and Social Psychology, 66, 1034-1048.	(Wegener & Petty, 1994)
	MLA	Burgess, Anthony. "Politics in the Novels of Graham Greene." Literature and Society, special issue of Journal of Contemporary History, vol. 2, no. 2, 1967, pp. 93-99.	(Burgess 94)
Website	APA	Purr, J. (2019). How to get certified. Retrieved from https://www.website.com	(Purr, 2019)
	MLA	Dunn, Sally. "Pass Your English Test.", www.website.com/ Accessed 5 August 2017.	(Dunn, "Pass Your English Test")

III. WRITING, SPEAKING, AND LISTENING

5. Characteristics of effective speech and presentation

Listening, speaking, viewing, and presenting are used in a variety of ways in the classroom. Students need to develop these skills in order to succeed in college and career. There are several effective and engaging strategies that teachers implement to teach speaking, listening, presenting, and viewing.

Speaking skills

Giving students formal and informal opportunities to enhance their communication skills is important. Below are some activities that incorporate speaking skills.

- **Speeches** (formal and informal)
  - Because many students do not like public speaking, the teacher should make these activities non-threatening and build students' confidence.
  - Teachers can help students develop eye contact, organization skills, vocal control, etc.

- **Debates (also effective for listening)**
  - When students participate in debates, either as a group or as individuals, they have an opportunity to use critical thinking and presentation skills.
  - Debates help students cultivate abstract thinking and build skills like citizenship, etiquette, organization, persuasion, public speaking, research, and teamwork.
  - The most important elements of a debate are a predetermined topic, opposing viewpoints, and arguments.

- **Gallery walks**
  - A gallery walk is an activity where students walk around class and visit different stations.
  - Students learn how to synthesize important concepts.
  - Gallery walks promote higher-order thinking, team building, and presentation skills.

- **Collaborative discussion**
  - Discussions can be teacher-led.
  - Students can engage in discussions in groups.
  - Students can discuss in pairs.

Quick Tip

To deliver an effective presentation, students should keep in mind these four criteria:

- Eye contact
- Pace
- Volume
- Inflection

Listening skills

Active listening requires the listener to fully concentrate, comprehend, and repeat back the information presented. Not only should a teacher model the active listening skill, but the teacher should also present learning activities to strengthen students' listening capabilities. There are several methods that can help students improve upon this skill (Burley-Allen, 1995).

- Create interpersonal activities such as student-to-student interviews.
- Create group activities where effective listening is the goal.
- Create audio and video stations.
- Ask students to paraphrase new material.

Barriers to listening

Several barriers exist when it comes to effective listening. These may occur at any stage of the listening process. Teachers should be aware of these barriers so they can help students be effective listeners.

Types of Barriers

Environment and Physical	Cognitive and Personal	Speaker
These barriers include outside noise as well as seating arrangements.	These barriers include the tendency to daydream, lose concentration, confuse the message, and even have personal biases about the speaker or message.	These barriers include when the speech is disorganized, difficult to understand, dull, and lengthy.

Presenting skills

Class presentations can encourage purposeful speaking and allow students to demonstrate content knowledge. Learning how to deliver complex information to others is a skill that needs to be cultivated. Teachers can ask students to do the following:

- Present with technology (i.e., multimedia presentation software).
- Integrate information from oral and media sources in presentations.

Quick Tip

As other students present, the members of the audience can:

- Write a response to the presentation.
- Ask relevant questions during the presentation.

Tips for teachers:

- Teach students about body language.
- Ensure students understand the purpose of the presentation.
- Allow time for students to plan and practice their presentation.

Audience analysis and awareness in presentations

As students prepare for presentations, they need to be able to adapt their speech and the presentation to the context and the audience (e.g., level of understanding, interests). Here are some key aspects to consider (Audience Analysis, 2019):

- Demographics
- Expectations
- Prior knowledge
- Audience size
- Setting

Viewing media

The use of media in the class can enhance learning and provide many advantages, such as increased student engagement, increased interest in the topic, improved critical thinking skills, and extended exposure to authentic learning experience. Additionally, media appeals to various learning styles: visual, auditory, and kinesthetic. Teachers can incorporate different instructional strategies to engage their students with media including:

- Analyzing the effects of techniques in the media.
- Comparing and contrasting the reading of a story to listening to an audio or viewing a video version of the text.
- Analyzing multiple interpretations of a story.
- Writing a response to art or other visuals.

6. Effective use of digital media to support and enhance communication

Integrating technology in the writing classroom can help teachers plan and deliver instruction that supports student learning, engagement, and motivation. Technology can serve as both a facilitator and a medium of literacy teaching and learning (Sternberg, Kaplan, & Borck, 2007, p. 420).

Technology	Description
Word processing software	This tool is best used for essays, reports, and other written documents such as résumés and cover letters.
Presentation software	Presentation software tool is best used for informational presentations where visuals are helpful.
Desktop publishing software	Publishing software is best for brochures, newsletters, cards, and small posters/fliers.
Blog	Blogs are best used for real-world writing that allows students to develop and hone their communication skills in an authentic way.
Document sharing software	This type of software provides many benefits to students including accessibility, immediate feedback, interactivity and collaboration, and engagement.

III. WRITING, SPEAKING, AND LISTENING

7. Research-based approaches to teaching writing

There are many approaches to teaching components of writing. Below are examples of commonly used approaches and best practices.

- **Discipline-based inquiry.** This is where pieces of writing are separated into distinct forms. Students focus on a specific form of writing and then investigate its individual parts. It involves higher-order thinking skills like analyzing and questioning to form conclusions about a piece of writing.

- **Self-regulated strategy development.** This is where the teacher provides background knowledge and introduces a form of writing. Then, the teacher models the technique and supports the students until they can perform the skill on their own (*I do, we do, you do* method).

- **Introduction-body-conclusion strategy.** This is an instructional strategy that focuses on the organization of student writing. This emphasizes the importance of the organization of an essay. It includes an introduction with a thesis statement, supporting details in body paragraphs, and then a conclusion paragraph.

Providing feedback

There are many ways to provide meaningful feedback to students about their writing. It is important to remember that feedback must always be specific, objective, and positive. Teachers should suggest revisions and fixes in the paper without discouraging students.

- **Rubrics.** These are scoring guides used to evaluate the quality of students' writing. Rubrics are instructional tools used to communicate meaningful feedback, convey expectations, and guide students as they write.

- **Margin notes.** English teachers will often write feedback in the margins of student papers. For example, if a student misuses a word or has an error in writing, a margin note identifying the error is appropriate feedback. Teachers should judiciously choose which conventional errors are most important and address those first. Too much feedback on one piece of writing can overwhelm students. Keep them motivated by focusing on one or two things in their writing.

- **Individual conferences.** This is when teachers meet one-to-one with students. This is effective because it is personalized and gives the opportunity for students to talk to the teacher directly about feedback. Whenever possible, teachers should use individual conferences.

- **Ending comments.** Unlike the margin notes, ending comments summarize the feedback and address the paper as a whole. Again, feedback must be specific and provide useful information to help the students improve their writing skills.

Think about it!

Remember, writing on a student's paper "Great job!" is not specific and meaningful feedback. A better communication of feedback would be, "Your purposeful use of transitional devices in the first and last sentence of each paragraph gave your paper a logical and easy-to-follow flow. Try applying that more throughout the essay." This gives the student a specific skill to focus on and repeat in other essays.

8. Assessing reading, writing, speaking, and listening

Student writing can be evaluated in numerous ways. Teachers should be familiar with the different types of rubrics used to assess writing.

Rubrics

These assessment tools can (and should) be used for three reasons:

1. Inform students of the expectations before the assignment is started.

2. Act as a formative self-assessment or peer-assessment tool during the writing process.

3. Act as a final evaluative tool for the teacher.

Quick Tip

Rubrics across the content areas should include a section for following grade-level ELA conventions.

Rubrics can be holistic or analytic.

- **Holistic rubrics.** Holistic rubrics are best for assessing the overall quality, proficiency, or comprehension of content or skills (Suskie, 2018).

- **Analytic rubrics.** Analytic rubrics are best for giving detailed feedback on a specific set of skills to assess strengths and weaknesses (Suskie, 2018).

Sample Holistic Rubric

Score	Description
Meets expectations	• Essay demonstrates complete understanding of the assigned objectives. • Thesis statement is original and clearly stated, and ideas are well-developed. Organization is logical. • Writing is error-free, without ambiguity.
Acceptable	• Essay demonstrates considerable understanding of the assigned objectives. Thesis statement is stated and somewhat complex and original. • Ideas are stated but sometimes do not support the thesis. • Writing has some errors.
Needs improvement	• Essay demonstrates some understanding of the assigned objectives. • Thesis statement is implied or barely stated. • Writing has many errors and is inconsistent and sometimes confusing.
Inadequate	• Essay demonstrates limited understanding of the assigned objectives. • Thesis statement is missing or too simplistic. • Ideas are missing or unbalanced. • Organization is not clear. • Writing is incohesive and incoherent with numerous errors.

Sample Analytic Rubric

Skill	1 – Minimal	2 – Meets	3 – Exceeds
Mechanics	Many spelling, grammar, and punctuation errors; sentence fragments; incorrect use of capitalization	Some spelling and grammar errors; most sentences have punctuation and are complete; uses upper- and lowercase letters	Correct spelling, grammar, and punctuation; complete sentences; correct use of capitalization
Ideas and Content	Key words are not near the beginning; no clear topic; no beginning, middle, and end; ideas are not ordered	Main idea or topic is in first sentence; semi-defined topic; attempts beginning, middle, and end sections; some order of main idea and details in sequence	Interesting, well-stated main idea or topic sentence; uses logical plan with an effective beginning, middle, and end; flow of ideas from topic sentence to details in sequence
Organization	Disorganized and confusing	Organized enough to read and understand the ideas	Organized and easy to understand

Effective teaching practices are integral in helping students develop as writers. While some strategies were previously mentioned, below are other useful instructional approaches teachers can implement.

Peer review

During the writing process, peer review is a useful strategy. It fits in perfectly between the drafting and revising steps. The role and purpose of a peer in this strategy is NOT to evaluate the writing. The peer acts as a reader to offer feedback on whether or not the author communicated his or her purpose with clarity. This strategy helps build reading, writing, and collaboration skills.

Note: *The peer review process must be carefully planned and facilitated to be successful.*

Teacher-student conferencing

Teachers might wonder how they will be able to find the time to pull each student to discuss his or her paper. Again, careful planning and execution are required. An appropriate time to conference with students is when teachers have them involved in writing centers/workshops. That way, the rest of the class is working on something meaningful and valuable. These conferences do not need to take up a lot of time. In fact, they can be 1-3 minutes.

Written comments on drafts

If the teacher marks everything on the students' essays with a red pen, the feedback can be overwhelming and ineffective for students. To avoid overwhelming students with too much feedback, begin with the most glaring issues. Offer specific, helpful, and encouraging feedback. Margin notes are perfect for this formative task. Formative tasks are used to monitor students' learning in order to provide ongoing feedback. The notes at the end of the paper are best for an overall impression or summative feedback. Summative feedback evaluates student learning at the end of a unit or a lesson.

Writing workshops

Teachers can use interactive essay workshops to help students understand the writing process and to teach them various writing techniques. The teacher should take the role of a facilitator during these workshops. Students' essays can be used as the basis for instruction and class discussion. When critiquing the essays, it is important to let students know how to respond to their peers' writing. Writing workshops are effective instructional tools, and teachers can customize them depending on the students' needs. To make the writing workshop engaging and interactive, teachers should follow these strategies (Dartmouth College, 2015):

- Review all student essays before the workshop.
- Before the workshop, provide clear instructions and convey expectations.
- During the workshop, be available to facilitate and guide the process, but try not to interfere as this process should be student-driven.
- Engage students in a discussion and ask them to provide feedback.
- Provide suggestions on how to improve students' essays.

Highly effective teaching scenario

Ms. Taylor wants to make sure every student in her ninth-grade English class gets specific verbal feedback on a piece of writing. She has pinpointed a few areas where all students are showing weaknesses in their writing and plans for writing workshop centers to address those issues.

Later, as students work individually to revise their essays, she calls each one up individually for two minutes to give focused and specific feedback. Instead of pointing out all of the errors each student has made, she chooses to address individual problems that are not being addressed in writing centers. She knows that students can be sensitive about getting constructive criticism, so she begins by asking guiding questions that will lead students to strengths in their writing. Then, she asks questions that lead students to weaknesses she has pre-identified. Together, Ms. Taylor and the students come up with plans to strengthen their writing, and they schedule follow-up conferences.

Assessments

By the time students enter secondary grades, they are reading to learn, not learning to read. However, are they reading on grade level? Can they decode and comprehend complex and subject-specific texts? Anyone can be a struggling reader if she is given an unfamiliar text with heavy technical jargon or literary nuances.

That's why it is important to continually assess students' literacy processes. This requires data collection. Remember, highly effective teachers use data to drive their instructional decisions. The following table provides some of the assessments English language arts teachers use to make decisions in the classroom.

Assessment Type	Definition	Example
Diagnostic	A pre-assessment that provides instructors with information about students' prior knowledge, preconceptions, and misconceptions before beginning a learning activity.	Before starting a unit on literary movements, a teacher gives a quick assessment to determine students' knowledge, perceptions, and misconceptions about the different literary movements.
Formative	A range of formal and informal assessments or checks conducted by the teacher before, during, and after the learning process in order to modify instruction.	A teacher walks around the room, checking on students as they read. She might also write anecdotal notes to review later to help her design further instruction.

Assessment Type	Definition	Example
Summative	An assessment that focuses on the outcomes of a program or lesson.	Midterms, final exams, grades in the gradebook
Criterion-referenced	An assessment that measures student performance against a fixed set of predetermined criteria or learning standards. Criterion-referenced tests often put students into categories (i.e., basic, proficient, advanced).	At the end of the spring semester, students take the state standardized tests. The state uses the scores for accountability measures.
Norm-referenced	An assessment or evaluation that yields an estimate of the position of the tested individual in a predefined population with respect to the trait being measured. Results are usually communicated as a percentile ranking.	The National Assessment for Education Progress, or NAEP, is an exam given every few years for data purposes only to compare students reading scores across the U.S.

Example question

After each new unit of study in English class, Ms. Smith gives the class two quizzes. These unscored quizzes are used to help students prepare for the unit exam, which is 25% of the final grade. Ms. Smith gives the quizzes back to students so they can see what they need to improve before the unit exam. Ms. Smith also uses these quizzes to focus her instruction on what students need help with to be successful on the unit exam. What type of assessment is Ms. Smith using?

A. Criterion-based assessment

B. Norm-referenced assessment

C. Formative assessment

D. Summative assessment

Correct Answer: C

The correct answer choice is C because the teacher is using the quizzes as informal assessments after the learning process in order to modify instruction.

The key here is to recognize that the strategies used to teach fiction are not the same as they are for nonfiction and vice versa. Students must also know how to distinguish fiction from nonfiction.

9. Effective oral communication in a variety of settings

Some students are brilliant writers but stumble over their words when speaking. Others can deliver a poignant speech or interesting presentation but struggle to place written words in an impactful manner. Like everything else, these skills must be modeled, practiced, and supported. Below are strategies to incorporate effective listening, viewing, speaking, and presenting instruction.

Cooperative learning

Cooperative learning is an instructional strategy that focuses on students working together to achieve a common goal. This process uses mixed-ability groups to increase all members' understanding of a subject.

It is important to remember, anytime you implement cooperative learning, all students must be accountable for their learning. Cooperative learning is not just group work where one student does all the work, and the others sit back and put their names at the top of the paper. Effective cooperative learning requires all students to participate and add to the learning experience. Examples include the following:

- **Shared reading.** An instructional approach in which the teacher and the students share the process of reading.

- **Guided reading.** The teacher provides explicit instruction to the students who are reading. This strategy allows students to comprehend text fluently.

- **Reciprocal teaching.** Students become the teachers in small group settings.

- **Literature circles.** These are small-group, in-depth discussions using a piece of literature or text. This activity is driven by student inquiry and reflection.

- **Socratic seminar (Socratic method).** This is a formal discussion based on a text in which the leader asks open-ended questions. Within the context of the discussion, students listen closely to the comments of others, think critically, and articulate their critical responses to others. Students learn to work cooperatively and to question intelligently and civilly. Socratic Seminars can be small-group or include the whole class.

- **Small group or partners.** This is an interactive activity where students work collaboratively during the learning process.

- **In-class group projects.** Students work together on larger projects. Be careful to ensure everyone has an active role.

- **Philosophical chairs.** This student-centered activity encourages students to listen and respond to one another. One objective of this activity is for students to be open-minded. Students participate in a respectful dialogue and provide evidence for their claims. The teacher should set norms prior to engaging students in this activity.

- **Conference.** This is an oral evaluation of what students know and are about to do. The teacher asks questions related to learning goals, and the student uses their class work, notes, and synthesis to demonstrate their knowledge and understanding. Conferences can be formative or summative.

Grouping

When students construct knowledge together, they are learning collaboratively. Group problem-solving, creating, and planning involves paraphrasing and adding on to ideas, defending claims, listening and responding to others, synthesizing and considering others' perspectives, and compromising for a better process and product.

The challenge of collaborative learning is picking the right tasks and teaching students the norms and routines of productive group work. When grouping students for cooperative learning, small groups, or remediation/enrichment groups, teachers can use homogenous or heterogenous grouping.

- **Homogeneous groups.** Everyone in the group has been identified as having the same learning need or are all at the proficiency level. For example, a group of all level 3 readers. Homogenous groups should be used to address specific needs such as reading fluency and comprehension skills. These groups should change regularly, always target a specific learning objective, and be reflective of the most recent assessments. *Maintaining the same homogenous group for a long time can impact student self-esteem and be counterproductive.*

- **Heterogeneous groups.** Groups are formed so that there is a variety of learning levels and student interests. For example, grouping students by a reading strategy, such as making inferences about character choices in a text rather than reading scores, will provide more diversity among the group members. Heterogeneous grouping should be used in most classroom activities.

Multiple choice tests do not effectively assess verbal, nonverbal, and auditory skills. Teachers must match the assessment to the task for authentic assessment. The instructional strategies discussed throughout this book, in conjunction with observation (informal), checklists (formal), or rubrics (formal), are relevant, authentic ways to assess the proficiency of these skills.

Assessing student progress is an important component of teaching. Teachers can use a number of different strategies to monitor and assess student achievement.

Informal assessments

Informal assessments, sometimes referred to as formative assessments and alternative assessments, are an effective way to understand student progress. With informal assessments, teachers can target students' specific problem areas, adapt instruction, and intervene earlier rather than later.

- **Oral assessments**. These are assessments that are conducted, either wholly or partly, by word of mouth. Oral assessments include:

  - Answering questions orally

  - Performances

  - Presentations

  - Role play

Quick Tip

Teachers often use oral assessments when working with English language learners (ELL). It is easier for students who speak another language to communicate through oral assessments.

- **Written assessments**. These are assessments where students write to communicate their learning. Written assessments often yield more information than a multiple-choice test. Teachers should use rubrics to assess written assessments. Written assessments include:

  - Essays

  - Lab write-ups

  - Letters

  - Journals

- **Performance-based.** These are assessments where students are required to demonstrate their knowledge and skills. Any time a student has to perform a task rather than simply fill in multiple-choice bubbles, it is a performance-based assessment. Performance-based assessments are considered **authentic assessments** and include:

  - Participating in a lab or experiment

  - Engaging in roleplay

  - Conducting a presentation

  - Building picture books

- **Portfolios**. These are assessments where the teacher uses a series of student-developed artifacts to determine student learning. Portfolios are considered a form of authentic assessment and alternative assessment. Portfolios offer an alternative or an addition to traditional methods of grading and high-stakes exams. Portfolios assess students' work over a longer period of time than a test (i.e., over the entire school semester).

Progress monitoring

Progress monitoring is when the teacher and the student track progress and modify instruction and behaviors to increase student learning. Students and teachers can progress monitor in a variety of ways including:

- Data folders
- Fluency checks
- Portfolios
- Conferences

Example question

Mr. Rodriguez is sitting down with a third-grade student as they look over the work the student has done over the last quarter. Mr. Rodriguez and his student then discuss short-term and long-term goals and a plan to reach those goals based on the data.

Mr. Rodriguez and the student are using a:

A. Portfolio

B. Rubric

C. Oral assessment

D. Criterion-referenced assessment

Correct Answer: A

They are looking over the work the student has done over time, which is a portfolio.

Quick Tip

Rubrics are used as scoring criteria to a performance-based assessment like writing an essay or constructing a project. Benefits of rubrics include:

- Clarifying the learning target beforehand.
- Guiding instruction.
- Making grading objective.
- Providing students with a self-assessment tool and a peer assessment tool.

10. Awareness of various perspectives, cultures, and backgrounds when reading, writing, listening, and speaking

Culture

Culture is a shared language, set of values, beliefs, customs, traditions, and goals of a group of people defined by ethnicity, religion, and nationality. Culture is not static and continues to evolve. For example, Native American cultures differ by region, tribe, urban, and rural communities.

Understanding cultural differences is important to understanding your students and supporting their success. Culture differences will impact how a child interacts with their peers and teachers. Effective educators consider the specific cultural differences in their school community. The following are some examples of how culture can affect how children learn.

- **Use of dialect.** Students may use a different dialect of English. They may pronounce words differently or have different names for objects in the classrooms or actions they observe.

- **Answering questions.** In many cultures, asking questions is a sign of engagement in learning. However, in other cultures, asking questions is considered rude or implies the student does not trust the teacher or person offering the information.

- **Eye contact.** In some cultures, it is rude to make eye contact with anyone in an authority position, while in others, it is rude not to. Consider that a child who is looking away when given a direction or asked a question may be showing respect to you as someone they admire and look up to.

Test Tip

When answering questions about cultural responsiveness in the classroom, be sure to select answer choices that reflect an ongoing approach to celebrating diversity. Celebrating Black History Month or Hispanic Heritage Month is beneficial to building a culturally responsive classroom. However, these happen one time per year. It's best to focus on everyday culturally responsive approaches, like continuously analyzing literature written by marginalized people or people from other cultures.

Socioeconomic status

Diversity is not always about the language students speak or the customs in which they participate. Diversity also applies to students' socioeconomic circumstances. Some students will come to school without having breakfast. Some students will come to school without basic necessities. It is the role of the teacher to provide effective instruction for these students. Taking the time to consider all aspects of diversity in the classroom, including socioeconomic status, is essential to being an effective teacher.

Here are some circumstances to consider:

- Assigning homework that requires computer and Internet access is not being considerate of students' socioeconomic circumstances because some students do not have access to these tools at home.

- Communicating with parents via email may not be most effective because not all parents have access to the Internet at home.

- Statistically, students who come from families with higher levels of education tend to perform better in school. Therefore, it is critical to support all students in becoming lifelong learners so they can continue the cycle of student achievement.

Prior knowledge and experience

Students come to school with a range of prior knowledge and experience. Culture, gender, and socioeconomic status are just some of the variables that impact prior knowledge and experience. Even children from the same family can have widely different perspectives and experiences before and during their academic careers.

English language learners

While students are going through these stages of language acquisition, they will engage in several processes where L1 (first language) and L2 (second language or language currently learning) merge and intermingle. Understanding these concepts will help you on the exam.

- **Code-switching.** This is when an ELL switches back and forth between L1 and L2 when speaking or writing. For example, a student says, "*I am going a la playa tomorrow.*" The student uses elements of English and Spanish when speaking.

- **Acculturation.** Acculturation is the social, psychological, and cultural change that occurs when a student balances two cultures. It is the process of adjusting and adopting the new culture. (Cole, 2019).

- **Assimilation**. This occurs when the original culture is wholly abandoned; the new culture is adopted in its place.

- **Transfer**. The replication of rules from L1 applied to L2. For example, grammar and even pronunciation will transfer from one language to another.

Caution

Avoid answer choices that promote an English only approach to teaching ELLs. Research supports the use of a bilingual approach. This means teachers allow students to use L1 and L2 when learning English. Teachers must also allow students to speak their native language when needed. It is helpful to think about all the learning happening in school besides language. For example, students who can discuss an idea in their first language typically can write about it more fluently in their second language. Just say no to English only practices on the exam and in your classroom.

Verbal and nonverbal communication

On the test, you might be presented with a scenario where you will be asked to determine how to modify a teacher's presentation to improve communication. Each of the modes listed below influences how teachers interact with students, colleagues, and parents.

- **Body language.** Posture, stance, how a person holds their arms, what direction they are oriented to, how someone sits, stands, moves, or even holds their shoulders.

- **Gesture.** A specific movement of the head, hands, arms, and body. The movement can be affirming, questioning, indifferent, or hostile.

- **Tone, stress, and inflection.** The way something is said, phrasing, expression, and volume of a question or statement that informs its meaning.

- **Eye contact.** What and how a person looks at someone. Eye contact can cue many intentions, including approval, intrigue, understanding, disdain, and enthusiasm. Lack of eye contact can cue disinterest.

- **Facial expression.** The emotions and intentions communicated on a person's face. Through facial expressions, a person can communicate a number of emotions without saying a word. Unlike other nonverbal cues, at least seven facial expressions have been proven to be universal (Matsumoto, 2013).

- **Personal space.** The amount of physical space needed to feel comfortable and confident to communicate with people. This differs depending on relationships, the intent of the interaction, and the cultures of the people communicating.

A new student in the class has very limited English proficiency. He does not attempt to answer questions and frequently seems distracted during whole group lessons and independent learning time. What can the teacher do first to help the student acclimate better to the classroom?

    A. Encourage him to follow the model of his classmates.

    B. Have a conference with his parents or family to explain the expectations at school.

    C. Give him warnings and use negative and positive reinforcement to help him learn appropriate behaviors in the classroom.

    D. Walk through class routines to demonstrate instruction and learning so the student can see the classroom expectations.

Correct Answer: D

A student who does not speak English yet will struggle to understand what is happening in the classroom. The teacher needs to explicitly communicate expectations and routines so the student can associate the words with her actions. The student can then emulate what the teacher is modeling. Answer choice A is incorrect because the student needs more explicit instruction. B and C are incorrect because these should never be your first resort.

This page intentionally left blank.

Example Questions and Answer Explanations

1. Which of the following should students consider when preparing to write?

    A. Subject, occasion, audience, purpose, speaker, tone

    B. Impact, reasoning, grammar, spelling, morphology, length

    C. Medium, structure, word count, philosophy, opinion, information

    D. Assessment, rubric, grade, objective, interest, characters

2. A teacher is working with students on the structure and organization of their essays. Which of the following should the teacher emphasize to students when working through their papers?

    A. Grammar

    B. Spelling

    C. Revision

    D. Prewriting

3. Ms. Johnson wants to assess students' writing based on specific criteria and skills. Which of the following would be the most effective assessment tool for Ms. Johnson to use?

    A. Holistic rubric

    B. Analytic rubric

    C. Group rubric

    D. Alternative rubric

4. Which of the following would be most effective in helping students avoid plagiarism when conducting research?

    A. Have students paraphrase and use note cards when researching information.

    B. Have students use quotations when taking information from the Internet.

    C. Have students use blogs rather than government websites when searching for information.

    D. Have students peer-review each other's outlines to be sure they did not copy information.

5. What point of view is most appropriate for expository and objective writing?

    A. First person

    B. Second person

    C. Third person

    D. Persuasive

6. Mr. Findley is a ninth-grade English teacher who wants to help students with the free writing process. He wants students to learn how to get words down on paper without thinking too much about structure or content. Which of the following would be the most effective tool in doing this?

    A. Word processing

    B. Document sharing

    C. Grammar check

    D. Plagiarism check

7. Ms. Ruiz is guiding students through a workshop activity so students can work together to revise and restructure their essays. She has students get into groups and begin looking over each other's papers. As she walks around the room, she notices students are reading the papers but are confused about how to provide feedback. Which of the following mistakes did Ms. Ruiz make that most likely contributed to the lack of students' understanding?

    A. She did not structure the groups properly.

    B. She should have grouped students based on writing abilities.

    C. She did not provide explicit instructions on what the students should do in the activity.

    D. She did not use a reward system for those who participated.

8. This strategy involves a formal discussion based on a text in which the leader asks open-ended questions.

    A. Philosophical chairs

    B. Literature circles

    C. Socratic seminar

    D. Formal presentations

9. Which of the following would be most effective to assess students' writing skills over a period of time?

    A. Research paper

    B. Writing portfolio

    C. Oral presentation

    D. Writing workshop

10. Which of the following would be the most effective activity to help students apply their non-verbal skills?

    A. Listen to a guest speaker on how she uses non-verbal skills in speeches.

    B. Have students act out a scene from a play without words, only using body gestures.

    C. Allow students to work in groups to discuss different non-verbal approaches in their favorite movies.

    D. Have students read a section in the textbook about non-verbal communication and answer comprehension questions.

Number	Answer	Explanation
1.	A	Think **SOAPStone**: **s**ubject, **o**ccasion, **a**udience, **p**urpose, **s**peaker, **t**one.
2.	C	The most important thing a teacher can do to help students understand their writing is to focus on revision. It is important that students understand that a piece of writing is only at the beginning stages after the first draft is completed. Effective writing takes several drafts and many revisions.
3.	B	**Holistic rubric**. Best for assessing overall quality, proficiency, or comprehension of content or skills **Analytic rubric.** Best for giving detailed feedback on a specific set of skills to assess strengths and weaknesses Answer choices C and D are nonsense answers.
4.	A	To avoid plagiarism, the teacher must focus on paraphrasing and notetaking skills. Notecards often help in this situation. However, this answer choice is correct because of the word *paraphrase*. None of the other answer choices help to reduce plagiarism.
5.	C	Third-person narrative is most appropriate for expository writing. First and second person are usually used in persuasive writing or narrative writing. Answer D is not a type of point of view.
6.	A	Word processing is the most effective tool in this case because students can free write using a blank document. Document-sharing software is an effective tool for peer reviews. Answer choices C and D are not applicable based on the goal for this activity.
7.	C	Before getting students into groups, the teacher should have communicated clear, concise, and explicit instructions to students. The students in this scenario do not know what is expected. This is problematic. Therefore, communicating explicit instructions would have helped students understand what was expected of them.
8.	C	The Socratic seminar is based on open-ended questions where students use critical listening and thinking skills to discuss important concepts. Within the context of the discussion, students listen closely to the comments of others, think critically for themselves, and articulate their own thoughts and their responses to the thoughts of others.
9.	B	A writing portfolio allows the students and teacher to evaluate a body of work over a certain amount of time. Students can look over examples of their writing and how their writing evolves as the school year progresses. The key phrase in this question that leads to portfolio is *over time.*
10.	B	The key word in this question is *apply*. The only answer choice that has students applying non-verbal skills is answer choice B.

III. WRITING, SPEAKING, AND LISTENING

Quick Reference Guides

Good Words List

When I build study guides, I identify what I call *good words* in the answer choices to determine correct and incorrect answers. Good words are terms and phrases taken from the test specifications that highlight best practices. If you see these words in answer choices on the exam, slow down and have a closer look. There is a good possibility these words are in the correct answer choice. I have also included a list of bad words and phrases to avoid. These are typically not the correct answer choice on the exam.

Good Words and Phrases

Accommodations. Modifying instruction or using supports to help special education students achieve. Accommodations do NOT involve lowering the standard or delaying learning.

Action research. The process of evaluating data in the classroom to identify issues and implementing effective and quick actions to solve problems.

Allocating resources. Portioning resources so all students have equal opportunity and time while balancing curriculum and instruction.

Assessments. Using formative and summative data to monitor progress and measure outcomes.

Authentic instruction. Providing students with meaningful, relevant, and useful learning experiences and activities.

Balanced literacy. Reading and writing instruction that uses a variety of literary genres including literary and informational texts.

Bilingual instruction. Helping students use elements of their first language to support learning in English.

Celebrate culture. Finding materials and resources to celebrate the different cultures represented in your classroom.

Classroom management. A variety of skills and techniques that teachers use to keep students organized, orderly, focused, attentive, on task, and academically productive during class.

Collaborative learning. These are strategies that are student-centered and self-directed rather than led by the teacher. Collaboration can also be working with colleagues or stakeholders to improve, create, or produce something.

Comprehensible education. Making information and lessons understandable to students by accommodating and using ancillary materials to help with language barriers.

Concept map. Visual representation of content. Especially useful for illustrating concepts like cause and effect, problem and solution, compare and contrast, etc.

Consent Decree. Protects students' right to a free, comprehensible education. It addresses civil and academic rights of English language learners (ELLs) and requires instruction be delivered in a comprehensible manner so all students can fully participate.

Critical thinking. Higher-order thinking skills that involve evaluating, analyzing, creating, and applying knowledge.

Cultural responsiveness. Instruction as a pedagogy that empowers students intellectually, socially, and emotionally by celebrating and learning about other cultures. This includes recognizing the importance of including students' cultural references in all aspects of learning and designing a productive learning environment.

Data driven decisions. Using scores, writing samples, observations, and other types of qualitative and quantitative data to make instructional decisions.

Depth of knowledge. Framework that is used to identify the cognitive complexity of a problem.

Developmentally appropriate instruction (DAP). Choosing text, tools, and activities that are appropriate for the students' grade level.

Differentiated instruction. Providing all learners in a diverse classroom with different methods to understand instruction.

Diversity as an asset. Seeing diversity in the classroom as an opportunity to learn new things through the perspectives of others.

Evidenced-based. Providing instruction using materials with the best scientific evidence available.

Follow the IEP. A student's individualized education program (IEP) is a legal document. If you see IEP in the answer choices, it is most likely the correct answer.

High expectations for ALL learners. Holding all students to high academic standards regardless of the students' achievement level, ethnicity, language, socioeconomic status.

Horizontal alignment. Organization and coordination of standards and learning goals across content areas in the same grade level.

Inclusive. Providing students with resources and experiences that represent their culture and ethnicity.

Informal learning. Supporting students with self-directed, collaborative learning outside of the classroom.

Interdisciplinary activities. Activities that connect two or more content areas; promotes relevance and critical thinking.

Intrinsic motivation. Answers that promote autonomy, relatedness, and competence are ways to apply intrinsic motivation. Be on the lookout for these answer choices.

Metacognition. Analysis of your own thinking.

Modeling. Demonstrating the application of a skill or knowledge.

Modifications. Changes to the curriculum and learning environment in accordance to a student's IEP. Modifications change the expectations for learning and the level of assessment.

Outcomes. The results of a program, strategy, or resources implemented in the classroom.

Performance assessment. An activity assigned to students to assess their mastery of multiple learning goals aligned to standards.

Primary resource. These are materials and information in their original form like diaries, journals, songs, paintings, and autobiographies.

Prior knowledge. What students know about a topic from their previous experiences and learning.

Progress monitor. Keeping track of student or whole class learning in real time. Quantifiable measures of progress, conferring, observing, exit tickets, and student self-assessments.

Relevance, real-world, and relatable. Be sure to choose answers that promote real-world application and make learning relatable to students' lives.

Reliable. Consistent. Producing consistent results under similar conditions.

Remediation. Correcting or changing something to make it better.

Rigorous. A word used to describe curriculum that is challenging and requires students to use higher-order thinking skills.

Scaffolding. Using supports to help students achieve a standard that they would not achieve on their own.

Secondary resource. These are materials and information derived from the original like newspaper articles, history textbooks, and reviews.

Specific and meaningful feedback. More than just a grade at the top of a paper, effective feedback includes positive aspects and how students can apply those positive aspects to improving. In addition, feedback should contain specific things the student should do to improve.

Standards-aligned. Ensuring that curriculum and instruction is aligned to the state-adopted standards.

Student centered/learner centered. A variety of educational programs, learning experiences, instructional approaches, and academic-support strategies that address students' distinct learning needs, interests, or cultural backgrounds.

Validity. Accuracy. How accurately knowledge or skills are measured.

Vertical alignment. Organization of standards and learning goals across grade levels. Structure for which learning and understanding is built from grade level to grade level.

Vocabulary in-context. Always teach vocabulary in context. It helps to relate the vocabulary to the real-world.

Wait time. Time between a question and when a student is called on or a response to a student's reply.

Bad Words and Phrases

Bias. Inserting personal beliefs, stereotypes, and assumptions in the learning process. This can also include learning materials developed from the perspective of the dominant culture that exclude minority perspectives.

Call the parents, principal, district, etc. You are expected to effectively manage your classroom without deferring responsibilities to others. In real life, teachers will often need to call the parents or principal. But on this exam, avoid answer choices that defer responsibilities to someone other than the teacher.

Extra homework. On this exam, students should be getting all of the instruction they need in class. In real life, we all assign homework. However, on this exam, extra homework is not the correct answer choice.

Extrinsic motivators. These are rewards of extrinsic value like pizza parties, recess time, etc. Students should be motivated by intrinsic motivators like self-confidence, sense of accomplishment, and feeling successful.

Hiring a contractor or external vendor. Anytime the answer choice includes using an outside resource like a contractor or a vendor to provide instruction or classroom management, this is typically not the correct answer choice. You are expected to be able to manage your own classroom using your own skills and capabilities.

Homework. Assigning homework is not a preferred strategy on this exam, especially when students are struggling with the material.

Homogenous grouping. Grouping by gender, English proficiency, or learning level is never a best practice on this exam or in your classroom. Homogenous groups should only be used in special circumstances and on a temporary basis.

Punitive solutions. Avoid answer choices that sound like punishments. For this exam, teachers are expected to be implementing positive behavior support methods so avoid any answer choices that sounds punitive.

Student aides. Using students as translators or support for special education or ELL students is never a best practice in the classroom.

This page intentionally left blank.

Literary Canon

Below is a list of many of the major works in the literary canon. Please understand that there is and will continue to be much debate as to which works should be included in the canon. This is not an entire list of every important work. However, these are the works you will most likely encounter on the exam.

Title	Author	Published	Synopsis
The Iliad	Homer	Around 762 B.C.	An ancient Greek epic poem in dactylic hexameter, traditionally attributed to Homer. Set during the Trojan War, the ten-year siege of the city of Troy by a coalition of Mycenean Greek states, it tells of the battles and events during the weeks of a quarrel between King Agamemnon and the warrior Achilles.
The Odyssey	Homer	Around 800 B.C.	10-year struggle to return home after the Trojan War. While Odysseus battles mystical creatures and faces the wrath of the gods, his wife Penelope and his son Telemachus stave off suitors vying for Penelope›s hand and Ithaca›s throne long enough for Odysseus to return.
Don Quixote	Miguel De Cervantes	1605	A noble (hidalgo) from La Mancha named Alonso Quixano, who reads so many chivalric romances that he loses his mind and decides to become a knight-errant (caballero andante) to revive chivalry and serve his nation, under the name Don Quixote de la Mancha.
Gulliver's Travels	Jonathan Swift	1725	An adventure story (in reality, a misadventure story) involving several voyages of Lemuel Gulliver. It has 4 books in all.
Emma	Jane Austen	1815	A novel about youthful hubris and romantic misunderstandings.
Frankenstein	Mary Shelley	1818	Tells the story of Victor Frankenstein, a young scientist who creates a sapient creature in an unorthodox scientific experiment.
The Count of Monte Cristo	Alexandre Dumas	1844	An adventure story primarily concerned with themes of hope, justice, vengeance, mercy, and forgiveness.
Narrative of the Life of Frederick Douglass	Fredrick Douglas	1845	A memoir and treatise on abolition written by famous orator and former slave Frederick Douglass during his time in Lynn, Massachusetts. It is generally held to be the most famous of a number of narratives written by former slaves during the same period.
Jane Eyre	Charlotte Bronte	1847	Follows the experiences of its eponymous heroine, including her growth to adulthood and her love for Mr. Rochester, the brooding master of Thornfield Hall.

Title	Author	Published	Synopsis
Wuthering Heights	Emily Bronte	1847	A man becomes obsessed with vengeance when his soul mate marries another man. Heathcliff is Cathy Earnshaw's foster brother; more than that, he is her other half. When forces within and without tear them apart, Heathcliff wreaks vengeance on those he holds responsible, even into a second generation.
The Scarlet Letter	Nathaniel Hawthorne	1850	Tells the story of Hester Prynne, who conceives a daughter through an affair and then struggles to create a new life of repentance and dignity.
Moby-Dick	Herman Melville	1851	A narrative of the obsessive quest of Ahab, captain of the whaling ship Pequod, for revenge on Moby Dick, the giant white sperm whale that on the ship's previous voyage bit off Ahab's leg at the knee.
Madame Bovary	Gustave Flaubert	1856	Tells the bleak story of a marriage that ends in tragedy.
Alice's Adventures in Wonderland	Lewis Carroll	1865	Tells the story of a young girl named Alice, who falls through a rabbit hole into a subterranean fantasy world populated by peculiar, anthropomorphic creatures.
Huckleberry Finn	Mark Twain	1885	Young Huck Finn, fearful of his drunkard father and yearning for adventure, leaves his foster family and joins with runaway slave Jim in a voyage down the Mississippi River toward slavery free states.
Dr Jekyll and Mr. Hyde	Robert Louis Stevenson	1886	A London legal practitioner named Gabriel John Utterson who investigates strange occurrences between his old friend, Dr Henry Jekyll, and the evil Edward Hyde.
The Call of the Wild	Jack London	1903	A short adventure novel set in Yukon, Canada, during the 1890s Klondike Gold Rush, when strong sled dogs were in high demand.
A Passage to India	E. M. Forster	1924	A novel set against the backdrop of the British Raj and the Indian independence movement in the 1920s.
Mrs. Dalloway	Virginia Woolf	1925	Details a day in the life of Clarissa Dalloway, a fictional high-society woman in post–First World War England.
The Great Gatsby	F. Scott Fitzgerald	1925	Set in Jazz Age New York, the novel tells the tragic story of Jay Gatsby, a self-made millionaire, and his pursuit of Daisy Buchanan, a wealthy young woman whom he loved in his youth.

LITERARY CANON

Title	Author	Published	Synopsis
Brave New World	Aldous Huxley	1932	Examines a futuristic society, called the World State, that revolves around science and efficiency. In this society, emotions and individuality are conditioned out of children at a young age, and there are no lasting relationships because "everyone belongs to everyone else."
Anthem	Ayn Rand	1937	The story of one man's rebellion against a totalitarian, collectivist society.
Their Eyes were Watching God	Zora Neale Hurston	1937	Considered a classic of the Harlem Renaissance, the epic tale of Janie Crawford, whose quest for identity takes her on a journey during which she learns what love is, experiences life›s joys and sorrows, and comes home to herself in peace.
1984	George Orwell	1949	A dystopian social science fiction novel about the consequences of totalitarianism, mass surveillance, and repressive regimentation of persons and behaviors within society.
Catcher in the Rye-	J.D. Salinger	1951	Details two days in the life of 16-year-old Holden Caulfield after he has been expelled from prep school. Confused and disillusioned, Holden searches for truth and rails against the "phoniness" of the adult world.
Lord of the Flies	William Golding	1954	Focuses on a group of British boys stranded on an uninhabited island and their disastrous attempt to govern themselves.
On the Road	Jack Kerouac	1957	Based on the travels of Kerouac and his friends across the United States. It is considered a defining work of the postwar Beat and Counterculture generations, with its protagonists living life against a backdrop of jazz, poetry, and drug use.
Things Fall Apart	Chinua Achebe	1958	Chronicles the life of Okonkwo, the leader of an Igbo community, from the events leading up to his banishment from the community for accidentally killing a clansman, through the seven years of his exile, to his return. It addresses a particular problem of emergent Africa—the intrusion in the 1890s of White colonists.
To Kill A Mockingbird	Harper Lee	1960	Takes place in the fictional town of Maycomb, Alabama, during the Great Depression. The protagonist is Jean Louise ("Scout") Finch, an intelligent though unconventional girl who ages from six to nine years old during the course of the novel.
Catch-22	Joseph Heller	1961	A satirical war novel follows the life of antihero Captain John Yossarian, a U.S. Army Air Forces B-25 bombardier.

Title	Author	Published	Synopsis
One Hundred Years of Solitude	Gabriel Garcia Marquez	1967	Tells the multi-generational story of the Buendía family, whose patriarch, José Arcadio Buendía, founded the town of Macondo. The novel is often cited as one of the supreme achievements in literature.
I Know Why the Cage Bird Sings	Maya Angelou	1969	Chronicles Maya Angelou's life from age 3 through age 16, recounting an unsettled and sometimes traumatic childhood that included rape and racism.
The Bluest Eye	Toni Morrison	1970	Tells the story of a young African American girl named Pecola who grows up during the years following the Great Depression.
The Woman Warrior	Maxine Hong Kingston	1976	Focuses on the stories of five women—Kingston's long-dead aunt, "No-Name Woman"; a mythical female warrior, Fa Mu Lan; Kingston's mother, Brave Orchid; Kingston's aunt, Moon Orchid; and finally, Kingston herself—told in five chapters.
The Color of Purple	Alice Walker	1982	Documents the traumas and gradual triumph of Celie, an African American teenager raised in rural isolation in Georgia, as she comes to resist the paralyzing self-concept forced on her by others. Celie narrates her life through painfully honest letters to God.
Beloved	Toni Morrison	1987	A novel based on the true story of a Black slave woman, Margaret Garner, who in 1856 escaped from a Kentucky plantation with her husband, Robert, and their children. They sought refuge in Ohio, but their owner and law officers soon caught up with the family.
The Joy Luck Club	Amy Tan	1989	Focuses on four Chinese American immigrant families in San Francisco who start a club known as The Joy Luck Club, playing the Chinese game of mahjong for money while feasting on a variety of foods.

Famous Works by Edgar Allen Poe		
"The Tell Take Heart"	1843	Describes the narrator's attempt to prove his sanity as he explains his meticulous plans for killing the old man only prove his madness.
"The Raven"	1845	Tells of a talking raven's mysterious visit to a distraught lover, tracing the man's slow descent into madness.
"Annabel Lee"	1849	Explores the theme of the death of a beautiful woman. The narrator, who fell in love with Annabel Lee when they were young, has a love for her so strong that even angels are envious.

LITERARY CANON

Famous Works by William Shakespeare		
Romeo and Juliet	1597	A tragedy written by William Shakespeare early in his career about two young star-crossed lovers whose deaths ultimately reconcile their feuding families.
Julius Caesar	1599	Depicts the moral dilemma of Brutus as he joins a conspiracy led by Cassius to murder Julius Caesar to prevent him from becoming dictator of Rome.
Henry IV	1600	Set amid political instability and violent rebellion, the play is naturally concerned with the idea of rulership.
Merchant of Venice	1605	Antonio, an antisemitic merchant, takes a loan from the Jew Shylock to help his friend to court Portia. Antonio can't repay the loan, and without mercy, Shylock demands a pound of his flesh.
King Lear	1606	A tragedy written by William Shakespeare. It tells the tale of a king who bequeaths his power and land to two of his three daughters, after they declare their love for him in a fawning and obsequious manner. His third daughter gets nothing, because she will not flatter him as her sisters had done.
Macbeth	1606	Describes the destruction wrought when ambition goes unchecked by moral constraints—finds its most powerful expression in the play's two main characters. Macbeth is a courageous Scottish general who is not naturally inclined to commit evil deeds, yet he deeply desires power and advancement.
Hamlet	1609	The play depicts Prince Hamlet and his revenge against his uncle, Claudius, who has murdered Hamlet's father in order to seize his throne and marry Hamlet's mother.
The Tempest	1611	A play about magic, betrayal, love and forgiveness. It is set on an island somewhere near Italy where Prospero, the one-time Duke of Milan, and his beautiful daughter, Miranda, live with a sprite called Ariel and a strange wild man called Caliban.

Practice Test

Practice Test

1. The text selection below is an example of which of the following?

    "O Captain! My Captain!" by Walt Whitman (1865)

    O Captain! my Captain! our fearful trip is done,
    The ship has weather'd every rack, the prize we sought is won,
    The port is near, the bells I hear, the people all exulting,
    While follow eyes the steady keel, the vessel grim and daring;
    But O heart! heart! heart!
    O the bleeding drops of red,
    Where on the deck my Captain lies,
    Fallen cold and dead.

    A. Sonnet

    B. Elegy

    C. Villanelle

    D. Epigram

2. An example of a protagonist would be:

    A. Dr. Frankenstein

    B. Pontius Pilot

    C. Lady Macbeth

    D. Hamlet

3. Which of the following novels includes themes about culture and identity?

    A. *Things Fall Apart* by Chinua Achebe

    B. *Anthem* by Ayn Rand

    C. *Lord of the Flies* by William Golding

    D. *The Great Gatsby* by F. Scott Fitzgerald

4. Which of the following novels are paired with the correct author? Choose all that apply:

    A. *Their Eyes Were Watching God* – Zora Neal Hurston

    B. *1984* – George Orwell

    C. *Animal Farm* – Virginia Woolf

    D. *Catcher in the Rye* – J. D. Salinger

    E. *The Scarlet Letter* – Arthur Miller

5. Which of the following novels is considered an allegory for McCarthyism, when the United States government persecuted people accused of being communists?

   A. *The Scarlett Letter*

   B. *1984*

   C. *The Crucible*

   D. *The Great Gatsby*

6. Why would the following poem not be considered a haiku?

   The waves break on shore

   White foam kisses the edge

   Each one brings a new.

   A. There are only 5 syllables in the first and last lines.

   B. There are too many syllables in the second line.

   C. There are only 6 syllables in the second line.

   D. There are 18 syllables total in the poem.

7. The following excerpt from *Their Eyes Were Watching God* is an example of:

   "Listen, Sam, if it was nature, nobody wouldn't have tuh look out for babies touchin' stoves, would they? 'Cause dey just naturally wouldn't touch it. But dey sho will. So it's caution." "Naw it ain't, it's nature, cause nature makes caution. It's de strongest thing dat God ever made, now. Fact is it's de onliest thing God every made. He made nature and nature made everything else."

   A. Dialect

   B. Line

   C. Theme

   D. Characterization

8. Mr. Smith's class is preparing to read a series of poems by Emily Dickinson. Prior to reading the poems, Mr. Smith asks his students to research facts about the author and the time period in which she wrote. As students are reading the poems, Mr. Smith frequently asks students how the writing might relate to Dickenson's life and time period. Which of the following critical approaches is Mr. Smith using to help students understand the poetry?

   A. Gender

   B. Biographical

   C. Feminist

   D. Sociological

PRACTICE TEST

Use the following poem to answer questions 9-10.

It is the Harvest Moon! On gilded vanes
  And roofs of villages, on woodland crests
  And their aerial neighborhoods of nests
  Deserted, on the curtained window-panes
Of rooms where children sleep, on country lanes
  And harvest-fields, its mystic splendor rests!
  Gone are the birds that were our summer guests,
  With the last sheaves return the laboring wains!
All things are symbols: the external shows
  Of Nature have their image in the mind,
  As flowers and fruits and falling of the leaves;
The song-birds leave us at the summer's close,
  Only the empty nests are left behind,
  And pipings of the quail among the sheaves.

9. The poem above is a(n):

  A. Haiku

  B. Limerick

  C. Epic

  D. Sonnet

10. The beginning of the poem uses what type of rhyme scheme?

  A. ABABB

  B. ABBAA

  C. AABBA

  D. ABACA

11. Which of the following is most effective when helping students understand the difference between denotative and connotative meanings of words?

  A. Give students a list of words, have them look up the definitions in a dictionary, and then use a thesaurus to find synonyms.

  B. Write a list of words on the board and create a two-column chart. On the left side, record the precise definition. Ask the students to discuss which of the denotative (precise definition) meanings they have used in a real-life conversation. Then, ask them to brainstorm a list of associations they have with each of the words written on the board. Finally, ask them to discuss how the associations and the actual dictionary meaning of the words differ.

  C. Provide the students with a teacher-generated handout that lists the words in a two-column chart, the left side with dictionary definitions, and the right with the emotional associations commonly connected with the words.

  D. Give the students a matching vocabulary test with the words in the left column and both the connotative and denotative meanings in the right column as answer choices to see if they can differentiate between the two.

12. The words *cache, browser,* and *dashboard* represent which of the following influences on the English language?

  A. Historic

  B. Cultural

  C. Technological

  D. Social

13. Which of the following resources is most effective when determining the correct use of a semicolon?

  A. Style guide

  B. Digital dictionary

  C. Etymology guide

  D. Thesaurus

14. Most of Edgar Allen Poe's works are considered:

  A. Modernist

  B. Realist

  C. Traditionalist

  D. Gothic

Use the following poem to answer questions 15-16

"Hope" by Emily Dickinson. Available on the public domain

Hope is the thing with feathers
That perches in the soul,
And sings the tune without the words,
And never stops at all,
And sweetest in the gale is heard;
And sore must be the storm
That could abash the little bird
That kept so many warm.
I've heard it in the chilliest land,
And on the strangest sea;
Yet, never, in extremity,
It asked a crumb of me.

15. How does the author convey meaning in the poem?

  A. The author uses metaphor.

  B. The author uses hyperbole.

  C. The author uses satire.

  D. The author uses onomatopoeia.

16. What type of figurative language is the author using in these lines when describing hope?

    And sings the tune without the words,

    And never stops at all,

    A. Metaphor

    B. Onomatopoeia

    C. Hyperbole

    D. Personification

17. This line from "The Raven" by Edgar Allen Poe uses which literary device?

    "Once upon a midnight dreary, while I pondered, weak and weary,"

    A. Internal rhyme

    B. Irony

    C. End rhyme

    D. Allusion

18. Ms. Salvador would like her students to make personal connections with some specific quotes from the autobiography entitled *Narrative of the Life of a Slave* by Frederick Douglass. Which is the most effective method to meet this objective?

    A. Double-entry journal with quotes on the left side and student responses on the right

    B. Narrative essay connecting one or more quotes to a personal event

    C. KWL chart reflecting prior knowledge and gained knowledge

    D. Reflective essay exploring the students' favorite quotes

19. Which African American writer is known for her poems, memoirs, and work as a Civil Rights activist?

    A. Nikki Giovanni

    B. Alice Walker

    C. Gwendolyn Brooks

    D. Maya Angelou

20. Which 18th-century British novelist used her fictional works as social commentary?

    A. Virginia Woolf

    B. Jane Austin

    C. Emily Bronte

    D. Anne Bronte

21. A piece of literature refers to *Jacob's ladder* when discussing the connection between heaven and earth. This is an example of which literary device?

    A. Hyperbole

    B. Metaphor

    C. Allusion

    D. Symbolism

22. Ms. Wong wants to read *Antigone*, a tragedy by Sophocles, in her tenth-grade English class. Which would be the best way to approach the reading of this type of literature?

    A. Round robin reading

    B. Readers' theater

    C. Silent, independent reading

    D. Read along with audio

Use the following passage to answer questions 23-24.

Despite its light-hearted and chatty tone, "Fire and Ice" is a grim poem that highlights human beings' aptitude for self-destruction. The poem is a work of eschatology and poses two possible causes for this: fire and ice. The author uses these natural elements as symbols of desire and hatred, arguing that both emotions have the capacity to destroy civilization itself.

23. The term *eschatology*, as used in line 2, most likely means:

    A. Writing about the end of the world.

    B. Writing about heaven and hell.

    C. Writing about desire and hatred.

    D. Writing about love and loss.

24. The first line of the passage indicates that the author:

    A. Is concerned about the mixed messages the poem gives to the reader.

    B. Is showing the juxtaposition of the tone of the poem to its actual meaning.

    C. Is angry that the poem is misleading to the reader.

    D. Is amused by the confusion the poem conveys to the reader.

Use the following excerpts from famous poems to answer questions 25-28

A. To be, or not to be: that is the question:
Whether 'tis nobler in the mind to suffer
The slings and arrows of outrageous fortune,
Or to take arms against a sea of troubles,
And by opposing end them? To die: to sleep;
No more; and by a sleep to say we end
The heart-ache and the thousand natural shocks
That flesh is heir to, 'tis a consummation
Devoutly to be wish'd.

B. Water, water, every where,
And all the boards did shrink;
Water, water, every where,
Nor any drop to drink.

C. Two roads diverged in a yellow wood,
And sorry I could not travel both
And be one traveler, long I stood
And looked down one as far as I could
To where it bent in the undergrowth;

D. I wandered lonely as a cloud
That floats on high o'er vales and hills,
When all at once I saw a crowd,
A host of golden daffodils;
Beside the lake, beneath the trees,
Fluttering and dancing in the breeze.

25. Which excerpt above shows irony?

A. A

B. B

C. C

D. D

26. Which excerpt shows a metaphor?

A. A

B. B

C. C

D. D

27. Which excerpt shows a simile?

A. A

B. B

C. C

D. D

28. Which excerpt is an example of dramatic monologue?

    A. A

    B. B

    C. C

    D. D

29. What is it called when an author strategically or purposefully uses specific words and phrases to suit the purpose of the piece?

    A. Satire

    B. Form

    C. Diction

    D. Imagery

30. The principal rhetorical device used in the poem below is:

    "Her hair as dark as midnight
    Sleek and wavy, trailing down.
    Her skin as pale as moonlight
    Projects a silvery glow all around.
    The night so cool and quiet,
    As the stars twinkle in the sky.
    And all of nature stands in awe,
    As this beauty passes by."

    Midnight and Moonlight
    By Kelly Roper

    A. Narration

    B. Definition

    C. Description

    D. Analysis

Use the following passage to answer questions 31-35

_____. These organizations take in animals of all kinds for various reasons and care for them until they are adopted. Many local humane societies are stand-alone, non-profit organizations that are not county, state, or federally funded. They also do not receive any funding from large national organizations such as the ASPCA. Instead, these local organizations rely solely on donations, grants, and fundraising events in order to provide for the animals. Volunteers are an asset to local humane societies that are non-profit organizations. Not only are volunteers needed for a number of jobs on site, but volunteers also play an important part of the humane society attaining grant funding. In order to receive grant funding, the humane society must show that they receive support in a variety of ways, which includes help from volunteers.

Local humane societies work tirelessly to provide medical attention, training, compassion, and a clean and healthy environment for animals, but they cannot do it without the support of the community. Fundraisers and community events help to support adoptions, secure donations, and increase awareness of the organization. No donation of money, supplies, or time is too small. From community outreach to grounds maintenance to cuddling puppies, there are numerous ways to volunteer or support your local humane society in their efforts to care for rescued and surrendered animals.

31. Which of the following best supports the central idea of this passage?

    A. Local humane societies are often non-profit organizations.

    B. Grant funding requires the applicant to show various means of support.

    C. Local humane societies rely solely on donations, grants, and fundraising events.

    D. A volunteer can cuddle puppies at the humane society to help provide support.

32. Which of the following would be the most appropriate introduction sentence for this passage?

    A. So many animals are left without a proper home to go to.

    B. A local humane society is an organization that fights for the welfare of animals.

    C. It is inhumane to purchase pets from breeders.

    D. Everyone should give a portion of their earnings to a humane society.

33. Which rhetorical appeal does the following excerpt target?

    Local humane societies work tirelessly to provide medical attention, training, compassion, and a clean and healthy environment for animals, but they cannot do it without the support of the community.

    A. Ethos

    B. Pathos

    C. Logos

    D. Pragmatics

34. This passage would be best suited for which type(s) of publication. Choose all that apply.

    A. Textbook

    B. Classified

    C. Brochure

    D. Website

    E. Magazine

35. This publication is used to:

    A. Persuade

    B. Inform

    C. Describe

    D. Narrate

Use the following passage to answer questions 36-38

Impeccably green mountains overlook a picturesque New England landscape as families gaze upon capped and gowned graduates sitting along mahogany benches. One cannot help but think of this scene as suited only for institutions of the academic elite.

However, a different educational success occurs in this part of New Hampshire, where students wear jumpsuits and study in cells.

Grafton County Department of Corrections in North Haverhill, 35 miles north of Dartmouth College, prides itself on the number of inmates it's able to graduate from the state's new high school equivalency test.

"A student is a student," says Stransky on how he views this unique student population. One such initiative is an alumni tutoring program, in which inmates who've earned their high school equivalency certificate help current inmates who are preparing to take the tests.

"I'm here only once a week, so that's a limited opportunity, but their inmate peers are here all the time and can provide continuous support," Stransky said.

Support for education success goes beyond those directly involved with the education program. Down to each correctional officer, everyone shares the responsibility to motivate inmates to enroll voluntarily and earn their high school equivalency.

"We want them to be a more prepared and better people when they leave the facility," program officer Sgt. Mark Deem said. "Confidence that they could achieve something really makes a difference on whether we'll see them again."

Inmates tend to gain a sense of purpose by graduating from the program, which has been shown to reduce recidivism.

"I have a completely different outlook on my future because there are more opportunities for me when I get out," Howard said.

36. The rhetorical strategy in the first line is used to:

A. Inform the reader about the prison.

B. Narrate the experience from an inmate's perspective.

C. Persuade the reader to have compassion for the inmates.

D. Describe what seems to be a university but is actually a prison.

37. The tone of this passage is:

A. Concerned

B. Optimistic

C. Cynical

D. Skeptical

38. Why does the author use this line in the passage?

Grafton County Department of Corrections in North Haverhill, 35 miles north of Dartmouth College,

A. To show that the prison graduates more students than Dartmouth College.

B. To compare the prison's educational program to that of Dartmouth's.

C. To juxtapose the prison to an Ivy League college for effect.

D. To show how different the prison is from the college just down the road.

Use the following passage to answer questions 39-40

Academic performance for American students has not increased for several years, and China is consistently outperforming the U.S. in multiple subjects. According to the most recent Program for International Student Assessment (PISA), China outperformed the U.S. in reading, science, and math. Experts say the scores on the PISA can be directly linked to a country's economic performance, so U.S. officials are concerned. However, officials cannot pinpoint where U.S. students are specifically lacking, which makes fixing this problem difficult.

39. How is information cited in the passage above?

    A. Direct quotes with parenthetical citations

    B. Generalization with no supporting document

    C. Direct quote from an expert in the field

    D. Summary of information with source mentioned

40. The following line is used to appeal to the reader's:

Experts say the scores on the PISA can be directly linked to a country's economic performance…

    A. Ethos

    B. Pathos

    C. Logos

    D. Pragmatics

41. "So never lose an opportunity of urging a practical beginning, however small, for it is wonderful how often in such matters the mustard-seed germinates and roots itself."

The quote above from Florence Nightingale is used to:

    A. Intimidate

    B. Inspire

    C. Anger

    D. Appease

Use the following passage to answer questions 42-45

Taken from *Great Expectations* by Charles Dickens

My father's family name being Pirrip, and my christian name Philip, my infant tongue could make of both names nothing longer or more explicit than Pip. So, I called myself Pip, and came to be called Pip.

I give Pirrip as my father's family name, on the authority of his tombstone and my sister – Mrs. Joe Gargery, who married the blacksmith. As I never saw my father or my mother, and never saw any likeness of either of them (for their days were long before the days of photographs), my first fancies regarding what they were like, were unreasonably derived from their tombstones. The shape of the letters on my father's, gave me an odd idea that he was a square, stout, dark man, with curly black hair. From the character and turn of the inscription, "Also Georgiana Wife of the Above," I drew a childish conclusion that my mother was freckled and sickly. To five little stone lozenges, each about a foot and a half long, which were arranged in a neat row beside their grave, and were sacred to the memory of five little brothers of mine – who gave up trying to get a living exceedingly early in that universal struggle – I am indebted for a belief I religiously entertained that they had all been born on their backs with their hands in their trousers-pockets, and had never taken them out in this state of existence.

42. The passage is written in:

    A. First person

    B. Second person

    C. Third person limited

    D. Third person omniscient

43. How does the author come up with the appearance of his father as being stout with curly black hair?

    A. By the way his father looks

    B. By the description his brothers make

    C. By the shape of the letters on his tombstone

    D. By his family name

44. What do the "five little stone lozenges" represent in the passage?

    A. The author's five dead brothers

    B. The mother's five sisters

    C. The author's imagination of his mother's sickness

    D. The father's dead brothers

45. The tone of this passage is:

    A. Extreme sorrow

    B. Somewhat detached

    C. Extreme anger

    D. Somewhat elated

46. The following quote came from which author?

A people that elects corrupt politicians, imposters, thieves and traitors are not victims, but accomplices.

    A. Virginia Wolf

    B. F. Scott Fitzgerald

    C. Langston Hughes

    D. George Orwell

47. Which of the following authors wrote about slavery and the emancipation of Black people?

    A. Fredrick Douglas

    B. F. Scott Fitzgerald

    C. J.D. Salinger

    D. Charles Dickens

48. The following quote would be considered what type of literary element?

We are living in an Orwellian society and Big Brother is watching.

A. Metaphor

B. Simile

C. Allusion

D. Personification

49. Which of the following graphic organizers would help students activate background knowledge regarding WWI before reading *A Farewell to Arms* by Earnest Hemingway?

A. A Venn diagram

B. A KWL chart

C. A plot diagram

D. A sequence map

50. A student is erroneously using the word *advocate* as a noun instead of as a verb in his writing. The best way to fix this error is to reference which of the following?

A. Thesaurus

B. Dictionary

C. Pronunciation guide

D. Etymology guide

51. In a ninth-grade English class, a small group of students display numerous grammatical errors in their writing, especially the misuse of parts of speech. For example, some students consistently use adjectives when the context calls for adverbs. What is the most effective technique for remedying these errors?

A. Use mini-lessons, conferencing, and individual assignments to address specific problems.

B. Direct students to label each word in a given passage with its part of speech.

C. Direct the students to look up each part of speech in their grammar books and write a complete definition.

D. Diagram sentences from their writing on the chalkboard and assign additional diagramming exercises.

52. Students in an eighth-grade language arts class are starting a lesson by learning new vocabulary related to history, specifically WWII. The teacher would be most effective by first:

A. Showing students what reference sources are useful for social studies research.

B. Providing students with a dictionary to look up words and write their definitions.

C. Using a cloze exercise to teach the vocabulary in context.

D. Surveying students to determine any prior knowledge of the WWII terms and concepts.

53. Students are working independently and are analyzing two different texts. They are finding similarities and differences while also constructing meaning from both texts. Which of the following would be an effective instructional strategy for analyzing different texts?

    A. Engaging in cooperative groups for dramatic retelling

    B. Using a Venn diagram to make inferences between texts

    C. Examining text structure and text features

    D. Using plot analysis charts

54. Analyze the student writing sample below and answer the question that follows.

    The dogs' on the beach ran wildly, ears flapping in the wind.

    What does this writing sample indicate to the teacher?

    A. The student has a firm grasp on the use of apostrophes.

    B. The student needs further instruction in plural and possessive nouns.

    C. The student understands how to indicate possession.

    D. The student needs further instruction in the use of commas.

55. Read the student writing sample below and answer the question that follows.

    The author of the novels follow the same theme in each one. Each one of her main characters come across problems that he or she needs to overcome.

    What should be the emphasis of the student-teacher writing conference?

    A. Subject-verb agreement

    B. Pronoun agreement

    C. Punctuation

    D. Sentence structure

56. Which is considered a reliable source for gathering research information?

    A. Blog post

    B. Editorials

    C. Answer forum

    D. Peer-reviewed journals

57. Which is NOT true of an explanatory/informative essay?

    A. It should include a clear thesis focused on the prompt.

    B. It should use narrative information to prove a point.

    C. It should communicate ideas without interjecting opinion.

    D. It should be supported with details such as facts and statistics.

58. Which of the following is an accurate way to assess where a student falls on the reading continuum?

   A. Silent, sustained reading

   B. Repeated, monitored oral reading

   C. Round robin reading

   D. Choral reading

59. Ms. Messer is planning an instructional unit using *The Iliad*. Based on previous formative vocabulary assessments that measured her students' proficiency using structural analysis to decode unfamiliar vocabulary words, she anticipates her students will struggle with the language. As a good first step to take before reading the text, Ms. Messer should

   A. Provide students with a teacher-generated list of complex words for them to reference when reading.

   B. Deliver explicit instruction on using context clues and signal words.

   C. Provide a list of vocabulary words and have students look them up in the dictionary.

   D. Deliver explicit instruction on breaking down words by their roots and affixes.

60. Read the student writing sample below and answer the question that follows.

   When I went on vacation last summer with my family, we rented an RV and traveled all over the United States. We visited the Grand Canyon, Yellowstone National Park, then traveling south to Las Vegas, and finally we ended up in New Orleans before heading home.

   What should be the emphasis of the student-teacher writing conference?

   A. Parallel structure

   B. Correct use of commas

   C. Subject-verb agreement

   D. Misplaced modifiers

61. Read the student writing sample below and answer the question that follows.

   The owner had to chase down her dog in high heels when it broke free from its harness and ran away.

   What should be the emphasis of the student-teacher writing conference?

   A. Parallel structure

   B. Correct use of commas

   C. Complex sentence structure

   D. Misplaced modifiers

62. Read the student writing sample below and answer the question that follows.

   Once I got my driver's license; my mom made me run all sorts of errands.

   What should be the emphasis of the student-teacher writing conference?

   A. Joining two independent clauses

   B. Joining a dependent clause with an independent clause

   C. Pronoun/antecedent agreement

   D. Subject/verb agreement

63. A teacher demonstrates how changing the phrase "inexpensive shirt" to "cheap shirt" communicates a negative meaning when describing the word *shirt*. The teacher is illustrating which of the following concepts?

    A. Denotative meaning of words

    B. Connotative meaning of words

    C. Morphology

    D. Negative tones

64. Mrs. Smith has identified a list of complex words from a particular text that are essential to student understanding. Of the following, which is the best strategy to help students comprehend the identified vocabulary?

    A. Allow students time to look up words on electronic devices.

    B. View a multimedia presentation that lists words and definitions.

    C. Complete a crossword puzzle that includes the identified words.

    D. Create an interactive word wall as a class.

65. Vocabulary instruction should include all of the following strategies **EXCEPT** which of the following?

    A. Memorizing definitions

    B. Providing multiple exposures and opportunities for usage

    C. Analyzing context clues

    D. Recognizing word relationships

66. While learning a second language, English language learners (ELLs) move through all the following stages except:

    A. Pre-production

    B. Early production

    C. Production

    D. Intermediate fluency

67. According to the World-Class Instructional Design and Assessment (WIDA), the educator's role in teaching English language learners (ELLs) is to do which of the following?

    A. Immerse the ELL in English as if he/she is already fluent in it.

    B. Ask ELL students to read aloud to improve confidence in the second language.

    C. Create an environment similar to the ELL's original culture to help the student feel at home.

    D. Create practices that capitalize on learners' assets, including cultural and linguistic practices.

68. Mr. Jones has several English language learners in his class. He notices that these students often have difficulty following directions for assignments. One of the best methods he can use to visually help these students is to do which of the following?

   A. Ask the students to start their assignment directly after he gives directions.

   B. Draw pictures on the whiteboard next to written directions.

   C. Require students to listen to directions and then immediately write them down.

   D. Allow students to ask a friend for clarification of directions.

69. To help English language learners become more fluent in reading, teachers should do all of the following **EXCEPT**:

   A. Provide an explicit model of fluent reading.

   B. Utilize the popcorn reading method.

   C. Include repeated reading of the same text.

   D. Provide performance criteria.

70. Maria is learning English as her second language. In an essay about herself, Maria wrote the following sentence.

   I have been to Miami in 2018.

   What type of common grammatical error for English Language Learners is this?

   A. Preposition

   B. Gerunds

   C. Present perfect

   D. Passive voice

Use the following sentence from a student's writing to answer questions 71-72.

Jake had few friends. Jake deeply desired a dog for his birthday.

71. The teacher wants the student to improve sentence variety in his writing. What technique can the student employ to enhance sentence variety?

   A. Use active voice to open the sentence.

   B. Use a dependent introductory clause to open the sentence, followed by an independent clause to close the sentence.

   C. Use an independent clause to open the sentence and omit "Jake had few friends."

   D. Use a description to open the sentence.

72. Select the best argument for asking the student above to use a variety of sentence structures.

   A. To entertain the reader

   B. To challenge the reader

   C. To add vibrancy and interest to writing

   D. To make the writing process more enjoyable

PRACTICE TEST

73. While a student is working through an assignment, she encounters a set of homonyms that are confusing. What should the student reference to learn more about the homonyms?

    A. Dictionary

    B. Pronunciation guide

    C. Etymology guide

    D. Thesaurus

74. Look at the sample sentence below. Which of the answer choices illustrates an improvement in sentence variety?

The dog had issues digesting food. I took him to a vet.

    A. Realizing the dog has issues digesting food, I decided to take him to the vet.

    B. The dog is very ill. I must take him to the vet.

    C. This very nice dog needs to see a vet.

    D. The dog is nice and has issues.

75. A cloze reading activity does NOT assess which of the following?

    A. Cueing

    B. Higher-order thinking

    C. Fluency

    D. Vocabulary

76. Which of the following is an example of a hyperbole?

    A. *She ran 100 miles per hour!*

    B. *She is light as a feather.*

    C. *The song was as sad as an old dog.*

    D. *The office is like a dessert.*

77. What is a phrasal verb?

    A. It is a combination of two or more words that give the location of something.

    B. It is a preposition and verb combined to create one word that has a different meaning than each of the words separately.

    C. It is a combination of a verb and a conjunction, and it illustrates a connection between two or more items.

    D. It is a word that indicates the action of something.

78. Choose the sentence with the correct use of a comma.

    A. The student, and his mother both love soccer.

    B. Before I left my house, I cleaned my room.

    C. I cleaned my room, because it was messy.

    D. Jack loves apples and, his wife loves oranges.

79. Which is the most effective way to teach grammar, usage, and mechanics to ensure student application of the skills?

  A. Using grammar worksheets

  B. Through online grammar games

  C. Through student writing

  D. Using skills drills

80. Which of the following is an example of a tier 3 vocabulary word?

  A. Isotope

  B. Perspective

  C. Evidence

  D. Orange

81. A literature teacher is introducing students to new vocabulary words that are domain-specific. What is the best approach he can take to introduce students to technical vocabulary?

  A. Focus on tier II strategies.

  B. Give students definitions of new words.

  C. Provide students with a matching exercise.

  D. Ask students to use the vocabulary words in context.

82. A teacher assigned an essay to her students last week. When the students turned their essays in, she noticed that most students were struggling with particular grammar concepts. What should the teacher do?

  A. Have students trade essays for peer review.

  B. The teacher should correct all the errors in the essays.

  C. The teacher should set 1-1 conferences with each student.

  D. The teacher should have a mini-lesson for the entire class.

83. The following sentence has what type of error?

  The student should go to their locker after lunch.

  A. Parallel structure

  B. Pronoun-antecedent agreement

  C. Punctuation

  D. Subject-verb agreement

84. A teacher wants to see if her students can summarize information from a complex piece of text. Which of the following is the best method to assess this skill?

  A. Create a PowerPoint presentation on summarizing.

  B. Work in cooperative groups to discuss the story elements.

  C. Ask students to read a story and highlight important information.

  D. Have students write a description of the story using 1-2 sentences only.

85. An English teacher introduces her students to persuasion prior to teaching them about the structure of persuasive essays. She wants to use photographs to illustrate the effects of persuasion on the audience. Which of the following activities should the teacher employ?

    A. Show photographs of people suffering from illnesses.

    B. Have students tell a story about a time they were persuaded to do something.

    C. Ask students to work in groups to create a presentation on the effects of persuasive photographs.

    D. Ask students to interview each other about the effects of photographs on persuasion.

86. A teacher plans a class debate. As students debate, the teacher will go around the class and take notes on how often students use vocabulary words from the lesson. This is an example of which type of assessment?

    A. Rubric

    B. Anecdotal record

    C. Diagnostic assessment

    D. Criterion-referenced assessment

87. An effective method to help students learn to properly cite sources is to have students complete which of the following tasks?

    A. Multiple choice exercise covering appropriate citations

    B. A mini research project that includes citing sources

    C. A quick review of how to cite sources prior to doing the research project

    D. Review properly cited papers as a class

88. A teacher is introducing a unit on arguments to her English class. She informs students that errors in reasoning in arguments that undermine the legitimacy of the argument are called:

    A. Judgment errors

    B. Illogical fallacies

    C. Evidence-based conclusions

    D. Logical fallacies

89. Mr. Smith has asked his students to complete a project on persuasion. One of the students, James, wants to convince the school to support his charity with a fundraiser. What should James do to accomplish his goal?

    A. Pass out fliers with information about the charity and a number to contact to donate.

    B. Invite a guest speaker from the charity to talk about the charity.

    C. Show the charity's accomplishments with testimonies from people who benefitted.

    D. Provide a list of names of the people who belong to the charity.

90. Which of the following would be most effective in helping students understand audience awareness?

   A. Ask students to write for a different purpose (i.e., to persuade, to describe, to tell a story).

   B. Ask students to interview each other about audience awareness and then create a presentation.

   C. Ask students to write about a personal experience in the last year.

   D. Ask students to create handouts of the entire presentation.

91. A teacher wants to give students an expository topic for their essay assignment. Which of the following is the best prompt for an expository essay?

   A. "Write about the best route to take to school."

   B. "Describe the scenery on your daily route to school."

   C. "Write about your position on whether or not a new route to school should be paved.

   D. "Write about a time you faced a challenge on your way to school. "

92. When providing feedback in the margins of a student's essay concerning the excessive misuse of the introductory comma, an effective statement would be which of the following?

   A. "This is the third time that you have misused this comma type in this paper."

   B. "Go back and review notes on this type of comma."

   C. "We have covered this in class. I will be taking off two points for this mistake."

   D. "Great use of complex sentences in this essay. Please be sure to use the introductory comma."

93. Which of the following essays most likely has an argument and a counterargument?

   A. Narrative

   B. Persuasive

   C. Expository

   D. Descriptive

94. Which of the following is the best source for writing a research paper?

   A. Going to the library and finding books published within the last ten years

   B. Researching blogs and paraphrasing information from the blogs

   C. Using a database and finding peer-reviewed journals published within the last five years

   D. Searching Wikipedia and copying the information into the research paper

95. Students are analyzing two proverbs from two different cultures. The American proverb is, "The early bird gets the worm." The Mexican proverb is, "Those who get to the well early have better crops." What is an appropriate higher-order continuation of this activity?

   A. Interview family members about other proverbs and then compare and contrast the proverbs from different families and cultures.

   B. Watch a movie about proverbs in different cultures.

   C. Copy proverbs and their meanings from both cultures and then compare and contrast the cultures' main tenets.

   D. In cooperative learning groups, identify proverbs in different stories from different cultures.

96. An instructor wants to show her students how text is organized in a print magazine. Which of the following is the best way to do that?

    A. Ask students to highlight the main ideas with one color and details with another.

    B. Explicitly teach the class about essay organization.

    C. Ask students to summarize the details and ideas from the text.

    D. Ask students to write an essay that will only be graded for organization.

97. A writing activity where students write about their personal reactions and ask questions about a passage is known as which of the following text response strategies?

    A. Think-pair-share

    B. Reading response journal

    C. Literature circle

    D. Jigsaw

98. While reading the novel *1984* by George Orwell, Mrs. Todd's class is struggling to grasp the complex plot of the book. One effective method that Mrs. Todd could use to help her students would be which of the following?

    A. Skim reading

    B. Choral reading

    C. Plot diagrams

    D. Round robin

99. A teacher wants her students to be exposed to literature from different cultures. What is the most important reason to include multicultural literature during instruction?

    A. To help students understand the differences between cultures

    B. To ensure all students can see themselves in stories

    C. To provide contrast to iconic American literature

    D. To satisfy the requirements of the standards-based curriculum

100. When students are analyzing meaning, intent, effect, and technique in media, they should be asking all of the following questions EXCEPT:

    A. What statements are supported by non-biased statements?

    B. How could the message be misinterpreted?

    C. Who is the intended audience?

    D. When was the publication date?

101. Students in Ms. Brown's class are analyzing a print advertisement for a new product on the market for teens. Ms. Brown asks students to determine the intended audience, advertising techniques, and expressed opinions to help students determine which of the following?

    A. If the ad is artistic in nature

    B. If the ad contains a valid message

    C. If the ad is selling a good product

    D. If the company is attempting to cheat consumers

102. One alternative assessment, or an addition to traditional assessment, that includes a series of student-developed artifacts to determine student learning is known as which of the following?

    A. Performance-based assessments

    B. Portfolios

    C. Journal writing

    D. Blog writing

103. Which of the following barriers to listening occurs when the speech is disorganized, confusing, dull, and lengthy?

    A. Environment barriers

    B. Physical barriers

    C. Speaker barriers

    D. Cognitive barriers

104. Which is the best software for publishing a class newspaper?

    A. Presentation software

    B. Desktop publishing software

    C. Word processing software

    D. Photo editing software

105. Students are preparing for a presentation on the most lethal diseases in the U.S. and would like to use pathos to appeal to the audience. What should they do in their presentation?

    A. Present facts about each disease in the order of death casualties.

    B. Show pictures of patients with the diseases and include excerpts from family members.

    C. Invite a medical doctor as a guest speaker.

    D. Give the presentation during the National Disease Awareness Month (NDAM).

106. Which of the following is the best way to assess listening comprehension skills in the classroom?

    A. Play an audio file and have students evaluate the speaker in the audio.

    B. Give a lesson and have students write down their feedback on the lesson.

    C. Ask students to create a presentation on listening comprehension.

    D. Play an audio of a short text and have students summarize what was said in the audio.

107. The following excerpt is from *The Tell-Tale Heart* by Edgar Allen Poe.

I then replaced the board so cleverly, so cunningly that no human eye—not even his—could have detected anything wrong.

Select the context clue type that is most applicable for deciphering *cunningly*.

A. Antonym (The author uses one or more words with opposite meanings.)

B. Synonym (The author uses one or more words with similar meanings.)

C. Example (The author provides one or more example words or ideas.)

D. Definition (The author explains the meaning of the word in the paragraph.)

108. A high school English class is studying Isaac Asimov's expository essay *Dial Versus Digital*. To enhance their understanding of the essay's structure, the students should:

A. Develop a plot summary after they read.

B. Construct a cause/effect chart as they read.

C. Write a character analysis after they read.

D. Take notes on the use of figurative language as they read.

109. A teacher is using the following objective for her English class: *Students will identify examples of allusion, archetype, assonance, diction, tone, simile,* and *symbolism*. What is the best assessment to test the students?

A. Ask students to provide a definition.

B. Give a multiple-choice test.

C. Give true and false questions on a test.

D. Ask students to match the term to an example.

110. Which of the following is a quantitative test used to measure the difficulty of a reading passage?

A. Common Core

B. Bloom's Taxonomy

C. FCAT

D. Flesch-Kincaid

111. One of the most effective and least threatening methods to practice reading fluency is which of the following?

A. Readers' theater

B. Popcorn reading

C. Round robin reading

D. Silent individual reading

112. Ms. Sim helps her students look for context clues to comprehend new words as they encounter complex vocabulary. To further help her students comprehend and retain the new words and meanings, she could do which of the following?

   A. Ask students to write the words and definitions on a piece of paper.

   B. Create an interactive word wall using new words.

   C. Highlight the words in the passage.

   D. Complete a matching worksheet after the reading session.

113. Having students paraphrase a passage during reading instruction helps to ensure that the students are able to do which of the following?

   A. Comprehend the passage

   B. Recite facts from the passage

   C. Follow along carefully while reading

   D. Determine the keywords in the passage

114. When the selected reading text is at the instructional level, students require which of the following?

   A. Independent reading time

   B. A more challenging text to build confidence

   C. Time to work on another activity and then return to the passage

   D. Scaffolding and support

115. After reading *The Scarlet Letter* in class, a teacher wants to assess students' understanding of hypocrisy in their own lives. Which of the following is the best strategy to do that?

   A. Watch a movie version of the book.

   B. Ask students to use dialogue journals to note down instances of hypocrisy in their lives.

   C. Put students in groups and create a presentation on hypocrisy.

   D. Ask students to write an essay on hypocrisy.

116. One effective method to activate students' background knowledge prior to reading about a new topic is to ask students to:

   A. Complete a KWL chart.

   B. Complete crossword puzzles.

   C. Quietly skim the passage to see if anything looks familiar.

   D. Outline the passage as they read.

117. When teaching reading comprehension concerning a cause-and-effect passage, teachers should alert students to look for which of the following sets of signal words and phrases?

   A. *For example, for instance*

   B. *As a result, if/then, because, since*

   C. *On the other hand, rather than, similarly*

   D. *First, second, last*

118. During a writing activity, students analyze text and discuss literary elements in the stories. While observing, the teacher discovers students' literary analyses lack details and support. What would be the best approach to this situation?

    A. Silent sustained reading

    B. Whole-class instruction

    C. Guided questions and feedback on their drafts

    D. cooperative learning

119. Which is the **BEST** assessment for a final draft of a research paper?

    A. Peer review

    B. Student-teacher conference

    C. Writing workshops

    D. Analytic rubric

120. A teacher asked students to read a peer-reviewed journal article and write a paper. However, the teacher wants to ensure that the students do not plagiarize in their essays. What is the best approach to take to ensure students do not plagiarize in class?

    A. Ask students to paraphrase direct quotations.

    B. Ask students to write down the main ideas of the journal article.

    C. Ask students to only use 2-3 sentences from the text.

    D. Ask students to paraphrase in an outline and cite information.

121. The teacher has assigned a research project. This project will take several steps over an extended period of time. What is the first step the students must make toward completing this project?

    A. Take notes

    B. Choose a topic

    C. Search for information

    D. Create an outline

122. A teacher has the students work in pairs and read each other's essays. Based on this activity, which stage of the writing process are the students most likely working on?

    A. Peer review

    B. Editing

    C. Formatting

    D. Revising

123. A student is writing an essay and decides the best way to convince the reader of the main point is to use a lot of evidence and reason. The student is using which mode of persuasion?

    A. Ethos

    B. Logos

    C. Pathos

    D. Kairos

124. Students are reading a text in an American Literature class. They monitor their own reading and use a pre-reading strategy to help with understanding the text. What are students doing?

   A. Using metacognition

   B. Scaffolding

   C. Focusing on accuracy

   D. Improving reading comprehension

125. While observing her students as they engage in discussions, Ms. Radcliffe notices that most of the class is not exhibiting nonverbal communication cues, such as making eye contact, gesturing, and nodding. Which resource would be best to show students the importance of nonverbal cues?

   A. Online video on the importance of nonverbal communication

   B. Scene from an appropriate movie with the sound muted

   C. Popular music video with lyrics displayed

   D. Short play that the students act out in small groups

126. Mrs. Valdez is creating a rubric for an upcoming oral presentation assignment. What components should the rubric address so the students understand the criteria for effectively delivering a speech?

   A. Appropriate pace, volume, inflection, and eye contact

   B. Thorough notes, visuals, audience engagement, facts/statistics used

   C. Audience awareness, knowledge of topic, facts/statistics used, volume

   D. Appropriate pace, knowledge of topic, audience awareness, visuals

127. Ms. Martinetti is introducing Socratic seminar to her class as a model for discussion of an informational text. Which guideline for responding should she include in her directions?

   A. Listen closely to others' comments and build upon those comments in your response.

   B. Find proof in the text to discredit the conclusions and comments of others.

   C. Raise your hand and wait to be called on before making comments.

   D. Summarize what you have read without adding personal opinions or bias.

128. Ms. Smith's seventh-grade students just completed PowerPoint presentations about their favorite authors. While each student was presenting, she graded the presentation with a rubric. Ms. Smith noticed that although the format, effects, and visuals were sophisticated and met the criteria, the class as a whole scored low on the conventions of the language section. What should be Ms. Smith's next instructional step?

   A. Give specific feedback on the graded rubrics before handing them back to the students and assign grammar worksheets as homework to practice those important skills.

   B. Focus on the success of the technology portion of the assignment and add in daily bell ringers addressing the English language conventions.

   C. Give specific feedback on the graded rubrics before handing them back to the students. Then, create lessons on the conventional issues she saw using examples from the Internet.

   D. Interrupt the student's presentation and correct him/her immediately so he/she can make the correction.

129. When engaged in formal text-based discussions, students should:

   A. Make eye contact, build upon the comments of others when responding, and refer to the text to support claims.

   B. Be cognizant of nonverbal cues, be open to other perspectives, and interject opinions and ideas when they come to mind

   C. Make eye contact, be cognizant of nonverbal cues, and wait for their turn to speak

   D. Defend personal interpretations of the text, use text evidence to back claims, and wait for their turn to speak

130. Which of the following clearly outlines expectations and should be given to students before, during, and after writing?

   A. Portfolios

   B. Peer-reviews

   C. Rubrics

   D. Worksheets

Answers and Explanations

Number	Answer	Category	Explanation
1	B	Reading	Elegies are songs or poems written to reflect upon a death. The elegy in the example is reflecting upon Abraham Lincoln's death. A sonnet has fourteen lines using any of a number of formal rhyme schemes. Villanelle is a nineteen-line poem with two rhymes throughout. Epigram is a short poem that expresses an idea in an amusing way.
2	D	Reading	Hamlet is the only protagonist listed. All the other answer choices are antagonists. **Protagonist** – The main character of the story, plot, or poem. **Antagonist** – The main foe or enemy of the main character of the story, plot, or poem.
3	A	Reading	*Things Fall Apart* is a novel about the intrusion in the 1890s of white missionaries and colonial government into tribal Igbo society.
4	A, B, & D	Reading	*Animal Farm* was written by George Orwell. *The Scarlett Letter* was written by Nathaniel Hawthorne. Arthur Miller wrote *The Crucible*.
5	C	Reading	*The Crucible* is a 1953 play by American playwright Arthur Miller. It is a story of the Salem Witch Trials that took place in the Massachusetts Bay Colony during 1692–93. Miller wrote the play as an allegory for McCarthyism, when the United States government persecuted people accused of being communists.
6	C	Reading	The second line of a haiku should have seven syllables. In this poem, the second line only has six syllables.
7	A	Reading	*Their Eyes Were Watching God* is known for its use of early 1900s southern African American dialect. Dialect is a regional variety of language distinguished by features of vocabulary, grammar, and pronunciation from other regional varieties
8	B	Reading	The biographical approach focuses on an understanding of the author's life and perspective. By having students learn about the author prior to reading and then referencing her life throughout the lesson, Mr. Smith is helping students relate the work to the author's life. The gender approach delves into the attitudes prevalent in a male-dominated society. The feminist approach evaluates literature through the lens of the female experience. The sociological approach evaluates the social context and influences on literature.
9	D	Reading	The poem has 14 lines with a rhyme scheme. Which makes it a sonnet.

Number	Answer	Category	Explanation
10	B	Reading	Using the last words in each line: Vanes – A Crests – B Nests – B Panes – A Lanes – A
11	B	Reading	This is the best choice because it involves the students. It is guided and can be monitored to make sure students are grasping the concept. It also incorporates the real world. Using a dictionary and thesaurus is OK, but not more effective than Answer B. In answer choice C, the teacher does the work for the students. Answer choice D is not effective in higher-order skills.
12	C	Reading	This list of words is common technology jargon.
13	A	Reading	A style guide is a manual that outlines the standards for grammar and conventions.
14	D	Reading	While Poe did have a few works that were about love, for the most part, he is considered a gothic writer. He used the concepts of terror, mystery, and the supernatural to bring fear and terror to society.
15	A	Reading	In this poem, Dickinson calls hope a bird (i.e., *hope is the thing with feathers*). This is a metaphor. Onomatopoeia is a word that imitates a real-life sound. Hyperbole is an exaggeration for effect (its opposite is an understatement). Satire is when the author is using humor and making fun of a human flaw, not to entertain or amuse the reader but to get the reader to feel contempt for the subject.
16	D	Reading	The author is giving hope human-like qualities. This is personification.
17	A	Reading	The words *weary* and *dreary* rhyme, indicating internal rhyme. End rhyme cannot be established in this example because there is only one line. An allusion is an indirect reference to a well-known person, place, or thing from the past. Irony is used to depict a sharp contrast between how things unfold and how they were expected to unfold.
18	B	Reading	A narrative essay is a personal essay, and in this case, students are describing quotes from the book to their lives, making answer choice B the best choice.
19	D	Reading	All of the women listed are African American poets, but only Maya Angelou's body of work fits all the components of the question, specifically her role in the Civil Rights Movement.

Number	Answer	Category	Explanation
20	B	Reading	While Jane Austen's novels might have seemed innocuous during that time period, she expertly used her fictional works as social commentary and criticism.
21	C	Reading	This is an example of a reference to a Biblical story. These allusions are used to connect the audience of the time to something they are already familiar with. There are three types of allusions: biblical, literary, and historical. Of course, when reading older pieces of literature, modern-day audiences may not necessarily understand the allusions, and building schema is often necessary.
22	B	Reading	Because *Antigone* is a drama, readers' theater would be the most engaging and authentic way to approach a whole-class reading.
23	A	Reading	"Fire and Ice" by Robert Frost is about how the world might end. In addition, eschatology is the part of theology concerned about death and the final destiny of humankind.
24	B	Reading	The critique in this passage shows that although the tone of "Fire and Ice" starts off as light-hearted, the message is quite grim and shows humanity's problems with self-destruction.
25	B	Reading	This quote describes the irony of being surrounded by a plentiful supply of water that you cannot drink.
26	C	Reading	The line, *Two roads diverged in a yellow wood,* is a metaphor for a choice in life. This excerpt comes from the poem "The Road Not Taken" by Robert Frost.
27	D	Reading	*I wandered lonely **as a** cloud.* A simile is a type of figurative language that shows a comparison using the words *like* or *as*.
28	A	Reading	This excerpt is from *Hamlet* and is one of the most famous dramatic monologues in literary history.
29	C	Reading	Diction goes beyond simple word choice. With diction, the author expertly uses words to create a mood or tone and express an attitude.
30	C	Reading	This poem uses description, specifically simile, above anything else.
31	C	Reading	The central idea of the passage is about the ways local humane societies are funded. We can eliminate answer choice D because it does not relate at all to funding. Answer choices A and B can also be eliminated because they are single supporting details about the main or central idea of the passage. Answer choice C is correct because it includes the supporting details without being too specific.

Number	Answer	Category	Explanation
32	B	Reading	Because of the second sentence of the paragraph, the only one that fits is answer B. Answer D is too strong for the opening line of this informational passage.
33	B	Reading	The words *tirelessly* and *compassion* are used in the line to appeal to the reader's feelings and to elicit an emotional response. **Ethos**. Appeals to ethics by referencing the author's credibility **Pathos**. Appeals to emotions by creating an emotional response to the topic **Logos**. Appeals to logic using reasons and facts. **Pragmatics** – does not fit here.
34	C, D, & E	Reading	This passage would be suited for either a brochure, website, or magazine.
35	A	Reading	This passage is used to persuade people to donate to the local human society. While the passage does explain and describe, the main purpose of this passage is to get people to donate money.
36	D	Reading	When the passage starts out, the description is that of a typical college or university, "Impeccably green mountains overlook a picturesque New England landscape as families gaze upon capped and gowned graduates sitting along mahogany benches. One cannot help but think of this scene as suited only for institutions of the academic elite." Later, the reader learns this is actually a prison.
37	B	Reading	Optimistic is the best answer here because while this is a prison, the inmates are working towards a better future. Also, recidivism is down because of the schooling the inmates receive.
38	C	Reading	The juxtaposition of the prison and the Ivy League school, Dartmouth, has the effect that both places, although very different, provide people with valuable education.
39	D	Reading	The following line is a summary of the information, and the source is mentioned. *According to the most recent Program for International Student Assessment (PISA), China outperformed the U.S. in reading, science, and math.*
40	C	Reading	The line links academic performance to economics, which is an attempt to get the reader to understand the severity by appealing to logic. **Ethos**. Appeals to ethics by referencing the author's credibility **Pathos**. Appeals to emotions by creating an emotional response to the topic **Logos**. Appeals to logic using reasons and facts. **Pragmatics** – does not fit here.

Number	Answer	Category	Explanation
41	B	Reading	The quote is used to inspire because it says that no matter how small an act is, it can have a tremendous effect. In a sense, she is telling people to do something, even if it is something small.
42	A	Reading	The passage is written in first person because it uses the pronouns *I* and *me*.
43	C	Reading	The line in the passage that explains this is: *As I never saw my father or my mother, and never saw any likeness of either of them (for their days were long before the days of photographs), my first fancies regarding what they were like, were unreasonably derived from their tombstones. The shape of the letters on my father's, gave me an odd idea that he was a square, stout, dark man, with curly black hair.*
44	A	Reading	The line in the passage that indicates the author has five little brothers who are dead is: *To five little stone lozenges, each about a foot and a half long, which were arranged in a neat row beside their grave, and were sacred to the memory of five little brothers of mine – who gave up trying to get a living exceedingly early in that universal struggle*
45	B	Reading	The author is oddly detached as he tells his story. While the story seems very tragic, the author is explaining it much like one would explain a normal family.
46	D	Reading	Orwell wrote about corrupt governments and societies, and he is quoted as saying this.
47	A	Reading	Fredrick Douglas wrote: *Narrative of The Life of Frederick Douglass, an American Slave* "Self-Made Men" – 1859 "What to the Slave is the Fourth of July" – Rochester, NY, July 5, 1852
48	C	Reading	This is a literary allusion referring to the novel *1984*.
49	B	Reading	The **K** in KWL stands for "what do you already know," which activates background knowledge or schema before reading.
50	B	Language use and Vocabulary	A dictionary will let the student know that the word can be both a noun and a verb. The dictionary will also provide examples of how the word is used in a sentence.
51	A	Language use and Vocabulary	In writing instruction, individual conferences help teachers give specific and meaningful feedback on errors to a few students. When in doubt, choose individual conferences when giving feedback on writing. Also, the question says that it is only a small group of students, which also makes A the best answer.

Number	Answer	Category	Explanation
52	C	Language use and Vocabulary	With a vocabulary question, look for the answer choice with the phrase *in context*. Vocabulary is best taught *in context*. Copying words and definitions from a dictionary is NEVER going to be a correct answer on this test.
53	B	Language use and Vocabulary	The keywords are analyzing two different texts. The only answer choice that satisfies this is B because it includes an analysis between two texts. This is an example of matching an answer choice with what is being asked in the question stem. Pay attention to keywords. Also, finding similarities and differences is a type of compare and contrast, which is best done using a Venn diagram.
54	B	Language use and Vocabulary	In this example, the student has not mastered how to make a word plural, as evidenced by the incorrect use of an apostrophe.
55	A	Language use and Vocabulary	The student in this scenario does not demonstrate mastery of proper subject/verb agreement. The student incorrectly matches the noun *novels* with the verb *follow*. The subject of the sentence, however, is *author*; therefore, the correct verb should be **follows**. In the second part of the sample, the student uses the verb come incorrectly. It should be *Each one* **comes** *across problems…*
56	D	Language use and Vocabulary	Answer choices A, B, and C allow anyone to post and can be full of bias and misinformation. Therefore, they are not reliable sources. Peer-reviewed academic journals are considered the most reliable sources.
57	B	Language use and Vocabulary	Narrative information, or storytelling, is not a component of informative essays. The phrase *to prove a point* in the question makes choice **B** the best choice. The other choices are true of informative writing.
58	B	Language use and Vocabulary	Repeated and monitored oral reading can help a teacher determine a student's reading fluency. Eliminate choice **A** because it is impossible to measure students' reading when they are reading independently and silently. Round-robin and choral reading are not accurate ways to assess individual reading. In round-robin reading, the reading is not sustained long enough to be an accurate assessment. It is also not a recommended practice because it puts students who may be uncomfortable reading aloud on the spot. It is impossible to measure individual student reading while the whole class is reading in unison, which eliminates choral reading.
59	D	Language use and Vocabulary	The keywords in the question are *structural analysis*, which deals with breaking down words by roots and affixes. While the other choices might seem appropriate, answer choice D is the best option because the scenario outlines structural analysis.
60	A	Language use and Vocabulary	The student in this scenario does not maintain parallel structure in this sample, making the message confusing. To maintain parallel structure, the student should write, "*We visited the Grand Canyon, Yellowstone National Park, Las Vegas, and New Orleans.*"

PRACTICE TEST

Number	Answer	Category	Explanation
61	D	Language use and Vocabulary	The placement of the modifier *in high heels* is incorrect, making it seem like the dog is wearing high heels. Always place modifiers next to the person, place, or thing being modified. The correct example would be to say, "*The owner, who was wearing high heels, had to chase down her dog…*"
62	B	Language use and Vocabulary	The student in this scenario erroneously uses a semicolon to join a dependent clause with an independent clause. A comma is the correct punctuation when the dependent clause comes before the independent clause. Semicolons are used to join two related independent clauses.
63	B	Language use and Vocabulary	Connotative meaning is a suggested meaning influenced by culture and/or personal experience. These implied meanings are figurative and subjective because of the emotions or associations attached to them by each individual reader or writer. Denotative meaning is the dictionary meaning.
64	D	Language use and Vocabulary	The most effective instructional strategy is collaborating as a class to determine meaning. Word walls allow students to determine meaning using verbal cues and context.
65	A	Language use and Vocabulary	All the strategies are effective in teaching vocabulary, with the exception of memorizing the definitions. Students need to use the words in context and recognize relationships among words. Equally important is being able to use the words on multiple occasions. Rote memorization is almost never the correct answer on this exam.
66	C	Language use and Vocabulary	C is not a stage of second language acquisition. Both choice A and B are part of the early stages of acquisition, while choice D is a later stage where the ELL begins to truly comprehend information.
67	D	Language use and Vocabulary	The educator's role is to design effective instructional practices that value the learner's assets, which include their cultural and linguistic background. Choice A would only confuse the student. Choices B and C do very little to help students acquire a second language.
68	B	Language use and Vocabulary	Choice B is the only choice that offers a visual aid to help the students comprehend the directions. Pictures are essential in helping students with second language acquisition. Choices A and C offer no additional clarification, while choice D may add to the confusion.
69	B	Language use and Vocabulary	Choices A, C, and D all support increasing reading fluency in ELLs. Choice B does not help fluency and can be potentially uncomfortable for the student. Popcorn reading is randomly calling on students to read at unpredictable times in the text. For those uncomfortable reading aloud, this can be stress-inducing.
70	C	Language use and Vocabulary	Maria is making a common ELL error that involves the use of a specific time reference (*in 2018*) when using the present perfect tenses.

Number	Answer	Category	Explanation
71	B	Language use and Vocabulary	Using an introductory clause followed by the independent clause would create the following sentence: *Because Jake had a few friends, he desired a dog for his birthday.* This enhances sentence variety by making two simple sentences into one complex sentence.
72	C	Language use and Vocabulary	Varying sentence structure makes the writing less robotic and more interesting than simply using periods to separate every independent clause. Transitions and complex sentences help to make the writing varied and sophisticated.
73	A	Language use and Vocabulary	Homonyms are two words spelled the same with different meanings. The best way to determine meaning is to reference a dictionary.
74	A	Language use and Vocabulary	By combining the original sentences into one complex compound sentence, the writer provides sentence variety.
75	B	Language use and Vocabulary	Cloze reading activity is a fill-in-the-blank activity. While it is ideal for vocabulary, it is a low-level activity that requires little rigor from the student.
76	A	Language use and Vocabulary	A hyperbole is an exaggeration for effect. Obviously, the girl is not running 100 miles per hour, but the exaggeration means she was very fast. Answer choices B, C, and D are examples of similes because they compare two things and use the words *like* or *as.*
77	B	Language use and Vocabulary	A phrasal verb is made up of a verb and a preposition to create a new meaning. Phrasal verbs include phrases such as *left out*, *held up*, and *send off.*
78	B	Language use and Vocabulary	In answer choice B, the comma is appropriately placed between the introductory clause and the independent clause. In all the other choices, the comma is used when it is not needed.
79	C	Language use and Vocabulary	The key word here is *application.* Teaching grammar, usage, and conventions in isolation is not effective. The best way to teach this is by using student writing samples so students can show the application of grammar, usage, and mechanics. Students learn best when they can apply their skills.
80	A	Language use and Vocabulary	Tier III vocabulary words are specific to a particular discipline like the word isotope in science. Tier I words are common words used in everyday speech, and tier II words are academic and not specific to a particular discipline.
81	D	Language use and Vocabulary	Teaching new vocabulary in context is always the best approach. The other answer choices are not as effective in teaching new vocabulary.

Number	Answer	Category	Explanation
82	D	Writing, Speaking & Listening	Because the entire class is struggling, the teacher should provide whole group instruction. After grading the essays, the teacher will be able to pinpoint common issues and reteach these particular concepts.
83	B	Writing, Speaking & Listening	The *student* is a singular noun, so it should be replaced with a singular pronoun. The pronoun *their* is plural; it does not match the noun. The sentence should read *the students should go to their lockers after lunch.* This is an error in pronoun/antecedent agreement.
84	D	Writing, Speaking & Listening	Answer choice D is the only option that includes students applying the skill of summarizing.
85	A	Writing, Speaking & Listening	The best option is answer choice A because showing photographs of people suffering from illness can be very impactful and can enhance persuasion.
86	B	Writing, Speaking & Listening	Anecdotal records are detailed, narrative notes on a specific event created by the teacher to refer to later. In the example, the teacher is walking around the class and taking notes (e.g., anecdotal record), which she will use later to determine whether vocabulary instruction was effective. Rubrics are generally used to grade assignments. A diagnostic assessment is a pre-assessment, providing instructors with information about students' prior knowledge. Criterion-referenced assessments measure student performance against a fixed set of predetermined criteria or learning standards.
87	B	Writing, Speaking & Listening	Answer choice B is correct because it requires application of the skill.
88	D	Writing, Speaking & Listening	Logical fallacies are claims that invalidate an argument; they are errors in reasoning.
89	C	Writing, Speaking & Listening	Providing accomplishments of the organization along with testimonials is an effective way to convince someone to support a cause, making answer choice C the best choice.
90	A	Writing, Speaking & Listening	The best choice is A because it asks students to write for a different purpose. Being aware of one's audience requires one to write for different purposes. For example, when writing a letter to a grandparent, a narrative is appropriate. When writing an op-ed for a newspaper, a persuasive or argumentative piece is appropriate. The other three tasks do not address audience awareness.
91	A	Writing, Speaking & Listening	Answer choice A is the best choice because an expository essay aims to inform the reader. Answer choice B is descriptive; answer choice C is persuasive; answer choice D is narrative.

Number	Answer	Category	Explanation
92	D	Writing, Speaking & Listening	Feedback needs to be positive and specific. Out of all the options, answer choice D is the best. Answer choices A, B, and C are not positive.
93	B	Writing, Speaking & Listening	While a counterargument is typically used in an argumentative essay, persuasive and argumentative essays are often referred to as the same thing. Out of the four options, the best one is answer choice B. Narrative essay tells a story; descriptive essay employs imagery to "paint a picture" for the reader; expository essay aims to inform the reader.
94	C	Writing, Speaking & Listening	The best resources for research papers come from peer-reviewed academic journals.
95	A	Writing, Speaking & Listening	Interviewing family members is the best answer because it brings the activity into the real world and allows students to bring culture into the discussion in an authentic way. All the other answer choices fail to connect the activity to real life. Real-world examples are always a good choice on these exams.
96	A	Writing, Speaking & Listening	Highlighting is an effective strategy for outlining structure. This is a visual tool, and it allows students to clearly see and identify how the text is organized. This is application of knowledge. Answer choices B and C are not effective in showing students the essay structure, and answer choice D is not correct because it asks students to write an essay.
97	B	Writing, Speaking & Listening	Reading response journals encourage students to write down their thoughts, feelings, and questions concerning a specific literary work. Answer choices A, C, and D are activities that rely on sharing information with classmates, whereas reading response journals are completed individually.
98	C	Writing, Speaking & Listening	Plot diagrams require students to plot or map out the key points that create a plot. Answer choices A, B, and D involve students reading the story without discussing or analyzing the plot.
99	B	Writing, Speaking & Listening	All students should feel represented in the literature available in the classroom. Paying attention to multiculturism is very important as a secondary English teacher.
100	D	Writing, Speaking & Listening	Media literacy simply means being able to identify different types of media and understand the messages that are being conveyed. All of the questions are important when analyzing meaning, intent, and effect except choice D.
101	B	Writing, Speaking & Listening	By having students analyze advertisements, teachers can help students determine what is a valid message and what is just noise. In the example, teachers may discuss answer choices A, C, and D, but answer choice B is the most important aspect of the activity.

PRACTICE TEST

Number	Answer	Category	Explanation
102	B	Writing, Speaking & Listening	Portfolios offer an alternative method for assessing students. Portfolios can include a variety of projects, writing samples, and assessments to demonstrate student growth over a specific time period.
103	C	Writing, Speaking & Listening	Speaker barriers occur when the speech is disorganized, confusing, dull, and lengthy. Environmental and physical barriers include outside noise as well as seating arrangements, distance from the speaker, and the ability to effectively see the speaker. Cognitive and personal barriers include the tendency to daydream, lose concentration, confuse the message, and even have personal biases about the speaker or message.
104	B	Writing, Speaking & Listening	It might be tempting to choose word-processing software, but publishing software has more features that make it a better technology than word-processing software for publishing newsletters and newspapers. Photo editing software edits photos, and presentation software is not used for publishing.
105	B	Writing, Speaking & Listening	Pathos appeals to the emotions of the audience, so the best answer choice is B because it would invoke certain emotions.
106	D	Writing, Speaking & Listening	Asking students to provide a summary of what they heard in audio is the most effective way to assess listening comprehension. Evaluating the speaker (answer choice A), providing feedback (answer choice B), and creating presentations (answer choice C) are ineffective ways to assess listening.
107	B	Writing, Speaking & Listening	The synonym *cleverly* comes before *cunningly*, which shows that cunningly means cleverly.
108	B	Writing, Speaking & Listening	The question highlights that the activity is to analyze text structure. Text structure refers to how a piece of text is written. Cause and effect, chronological, and descriptive are all examples of text structure. Choice B is the only one that indicates text structure.
109	D	Writing, Speaking & Listening	The verb in the objective is to identify. Matching the literary elements to their example is identifying.
110	D	Writing, Speaking & Listening	The Flesch-Kincaid is designed specifically to measure the difficulty of a passage. Answer choices A, B, and C are not related to diagnosing the difficulty or readability of text.
111	A	Writing, Speaking & Listening	Readers' theater is a non-threatening method for students to read aloud by acting out pieces of the text. Answer choices B and C tend to put students on the spot to read aloud in class, which can be threatening. Answer choice D does not measure fluency.

PRACTICE TEST

Number	Answer	Category	Explanation
112	B	Writing, Speaking & Listening	Interactive word walls are effective tools for learning new vocabulary. Students get up and choose words from the wall in different activities. Answer choice A, having students copy definitions from the dictionary, is the least effective strategy for learning new vocabulary. A matching exercise is asking students to recall—a low-level skill. Highlighting words in the passage is not as effective as the interactive word wall.
113	A	Writing, Speaking & Listening	Paraphrasing is effective in measuring student comprehension because the student is asked to reword the passage.
114	D	Writing, Speaking & Listening	At the instructional level, students still need support from the teacher. They require the use of scaffolding and support to help with comprehension. Answer choices A and B will add to the frustration, while answer choice C only offers a distraction.
115	B	Writing, Speaking & Listening	Dialogue journals provide a method for students to thoughtfully explore their reactions and feelings concerning a text. Teachers can easily offer feedback as well as measure student understanding. These journals are also private, allowing students to share more than they might in a group.
116	A	Writing, Speaking & Listening	KWL charts are effective in helping the teacher determine students' background knowledge by asking students to state what they already know (K), what they want to know (W), and later, what they learned (L). The *K* in the KWL chart aligns with students' background knowledge. Answer choices B, C, and D do not offer nearly this amount of information concerning background knowledge.
117	B	Writing, Speaking & Listening	Each type of text structure contains signal words that identify the text's purpose. The cause-and-effect structure often contains signal words such as *as a result, if then,* and *because.* Answer choice A lists descriptive words, answer choice C lists compare/contrast words, and answer choice D lists chronological words.
118	C	Writing, Speaking & Listening	Engaging in a literary analysis is a critical thinking skill. Therefore, question generation and specific feedback on drafts are most effective. The other answer choices do not address high-order skills.
119	D	Writing, Speaking & Listening	Research papers are best assessed with an analytic rubric that addresses the various components/criteria of the project, such as the research process, the writing, and the citations. All the other answer choices—peer review, student-teacher conferences, and writing workshops—are used during the drafting and revision stages and are not assessments.
120	D	Writing, Speaking & Listening	Answer choice D has all of the appropriate steps when engaging in research. Ideas should be paraphrased and also cited.

Number	Answer	Category	Explanation
121	B	Writing, Speaking & Listening	During the research process, students must first identify a topic for the project. Second, students search for information. Third, students locate source materials. The fourth step is to evaluate the sources for reliability and validity. The fifth step is to take notes, and the sixth step is to produce the paper.
122	A	Writing, Speaking & Listening	Peer review is the third step in the writing process, and it occurs after students have drafted their writing. Students read each other's papers for clarity and purpose.
123	B	Writing, Speaking & Listening	In this example, the writer is appealing to the audience by using logos (logic). Writers appeal to the audience through ethos (ethics), logos (logic), or pathos (emotions). Kairos is knowing what is most appropriate (e.g., saying the right thing at the right time).
124	A	Writing, Speaking & Listening	Metacognition is being aware of one's own thought process. When students have metacognition, they understand the processes in their minds and can employ a variety of techniques to understand text. In this case, students monitor their own reading process, which is metacognition.
125	B	Writing, Speaking & Listening	Using a short clip from a movie with the sound muted would help students see the importance of nonverbal cues such as gestures and facial expressions. Students can pick up the tone of the scene through this activity.
126	A	Writing, Speaking & Listening	Answer choice A has all the components of oral presentation. Because the assessment is on the actual *delivery* of the speech, these components are the priority. The other criteria assess the preparation more than the delivery.
127	A	Writing, Speaking & Listening	One of the most important components of the Socratic seminar is that students acknowledge and build upon the comments of others. Socratic Seminar does not require or recommend students raise their hands to respond. This discussion model is also not a debate, so proving others "wrong" is not the correct choice.
128	C	Writing, Speaking & Listening	The best option is C—provide specific feedback and then create a lesson for the entire class and address the issue. If students do not understand something, adding worksheets as homework is not the best way to ensure they will learn it, eliminating choice A. Although having bell ringers for grammar is not a bad idea, if the students do not know why they are doing them or lack a frame of reference, bell ringers are not effective. Eliminate choice D because students should never be interrupted and corrected in front of the whole class; this could be very embarrassing for the student.

Number	Answer	Category	Explanation
129	A	Writing, Speaking & Listening	Answer A has all of the important components of text-based discussion. The most important thing students must do in this activity is refer to the text to support claims. Therefore, any answer choice missing that piece should be eliminated. The other essential component answer A has is building upon the comments of others. This makes A the best answer choice.
130	C	Writing, Speaking & Listening	Rubrics are assessment tools that help teachers grade essays and outline clear expectations for students. Giving students the rubric before writing takes place to set expectations, during writing to check expectations, and after the writing for feedback helps to set students up for success.

PRACTICE TEST

Analysis – Constructed Response

Analysis – Constructed Response

The constructed response section of the Praxis English Language Arts Content and Analysis test can be challenging. It is important that you use our suggestions and strategies below. Remember, this is not just an essay explaining a poem or work. It is a critical analysis of a poem or work. The graders are English teachers who are looking for you to do more than just summarize in your responses. You must think like an English major when writing for this exam. The following techniques will help you do that.

How long is the constructed response portion of the test?

You only have 30 minutes for both of the constructed responses you will be required to write for this exam. That means you must be strategic in order to read the poem or work, plan, write, proof, revise, and complete your responses in the allotted time. We recommend practicing so you do not waste time getting acclimated with this process on test day.

How are the constructed response questions structured?

You will be provided a piece of text or poetry, and then you will be required to complete the analysis task. The task will be specific in terms of what you need to do in your response. Stick to the task; there is no need for extra information or analysis. Just do what the task asks you to do. Below are a few examples of typical tasks for the constructed response section of the Praxis 5039.

- Read the following passage. Then using at least two examples from the passage, describe how the author uses imagery to develop the mood or setting.

- Read the following passage. Then in your own words, describe the central idea of the piece and how the author's use of figurative language clarifies and supports the main idea. Use specific examples from the passage to support your analysis.

- Read the passage and write a brief response for the following:

  1. Identify the point of view of the excerpt.

  2. Using specific references to the excerpt, describe how the point of view develops the characterization of the protagonist as an unreliable narrator.

  3. Analyze how the characterization of the protagonist will most likely affect the reader.

Test Tip

Notice that in all of these constructed response tasks, you are given specific instructions. Be sure to complete these instructions, nothing more, nothing less.

IMPORTANT

The 2 constructed responses are always structured in the same way: one will require you to interpret literature, and the other will require you to evaluate rhetorical features. Notice in the test blueprint that one constructed response comes from the reading content category (analyzing literature), and the other constructed response comes from the writing, speaking and listening content category (evaluating rhetorical features). The test will always follow this pattern.

Test at a Glance	
Test Name	English Language Arts: Content and Analysis
Test Code	5039
Time	3 hours – 150 minutes for the selected-response (SR) and *30 minutes for constructed response (CR) section*
Number of Questions	130 SR questions and *2 CR*
Format	Single selection, multiple selection, selected response, order/ match, audio stimulus, video stimulus, table/grid, and select in passage
Test Delivery	Computer delivered

Content Category	**Approx. Number of Questions**	**Approx. Percentage of Exam**

I. Reading
  A. Literature
  B. Informational Text and Rhetoric
	48 SR and 1 CR	40%

II. Language Use and Vocabulary	33 SR	19%
III. Writing, Speaking, and Listening	49 SR and 1 CR	41%

Pie chart: III. 41%, I. 40%, II. 19%

ANALYSIS – CONSTRUCTED RESPONSE

How is the constructed response scored?

You will be given two constructed response tasks. You can receive a total of 3 points per response. That means there are 6 points up for grabs in this section. It is not difficult to score a 3 on each response as long as you complete the task you are given.

Below is the scoring rubric for a score of 3. Focus on the elements outlined below when you are practicing and evaluating your writing. Read your essay back to yourself and check it against the rubric below. Sharpen the areas where you fall short.

Score of 3 – The response demonstrates a thorough understanding of content.

- Analyzes the specified elements in the selection accurately with some depth.

- Shows sound understanding of the selection.

- Supports points with appropriate examples from the selection and explains how the examples support the points.

- Is coherent and demonstrates control of language, including diction and syntax.

- Demonstrates facility with the conventions of standard written English.

What should my constructed response include?

Using the previous ETS rubric for passing a score of 3, you should make sure you have the following:

- **Completion of the task.** Immediately answer the question(s) or complete the responses outlined in the task. You do not need an introduction paragraph or conclusion. All you have to do is complete the task. Be concise; do not add any extras. Make it easy on the grader to locate your answers to the specific task outlined in the question.

- **Analysis.** Avoid simply summarizing the passage or poem. That is not the task. The task is to find meaning and use a critical approach to explain that meaning. Think like an English major and analyze the work using a critical approach.

- **Details and support.** Avoid generalizations. Use tangible ideas and images to explain the poem or passage. Be specific about what the author is trying to say in the poem or work.

- **Word choice.** Use vocabulary accurately to express your ideas. If you are not 100% sure of how to use a word or what it means, do not use it.

- **Grammar and mechanics.** This is a test to become an English teacher at the secondary level. You must have a command of grammar and mechanics.

What are some recommended study tips?

1. Read more literature and poetry and analyze the main ideas, figurative language, and other elements that provide meaning in the text. This can be simply reading a poem each day or a piece of literary work. Quickly analyze it and see how you may take a critical approach to the work.

2. Practice writing using the scoring rubric.

3. Use the scoring rubric to rate your own writing. Read your constructed response back and use the rubric as a check list. Ask yourself:

   - Did I complete the entire task?

   - Does my response indicate that I have a thorough understanding of the piece?

   - Are my grammar and conventions coherent?

4. Review, revise, and rewrite. All writers, even the most prolific, have to revise their writing. In addition, every writer has to practice in order to become proficient.

Using a critical approach

The most important style choice you can make in this task is to use a critical approach. A critical approach requires you to analyze the poem or literary work through a critical lens and identify meaning where it is not explicitly stated. Meaning can come from a variety of areas—gender, class, society, race, etc.

Identifying images or elements in the piece that convey meaning will help to increase your score. For example, water will often represent forgiveness, baptism, and rebirth. Elements of nature can often convey meaning in life and death. See the table for more elements and their meaning. Whatever you choose to analyze, be sure to support those observations with tangible examples in the text.

Sample Elements in Literature

Element	Meaning
serpent	the devil or deception
candle	light in darkness
dove	purity or simplicity
window	freedom
rain	sadness
fire	death or pain
apple	temptation

Be able to identify common figurative language.

Here is a table containing common figurative language in literature. This comes from content category one in the study guide. We've shortened it to include the most common figurative elements. You will want to choose from figurative language you are most familiar with, so your constructed response is accurate and demonstrates and understanding of the literary work.

Device	Definition	Example
Allegory	This is when ideas are used to symbolize people.	The *Hunger Games* is an allegory for humans' obsession with reality TV.
Alliteration	This is the repetition of a consonant sound at the beginning of a word for effect (e.g., sense and sensibility).	"She sells seashells by the sea-shore."

Device	Definition	Example
Allusion	This is a reference to a famous or well-known event or piece of literature to allow the reader to make a connection. There are three types of illusion: biblical, literary, and historical.	"I had no idea my comment would open Pandora's box." "He nailed himself to the cross with that statement." "It was like World War II in our house for years."
Archetypal elements	This is a character that represents some universal patterns. For example, all villains and heroes have certain characteristics. This rhetorical device is often found in myth genres.	*Garden* symbolizes love and fertility. *Light* symbolizes hope.
Assonance	This is the repetition of vowel sounds to create internal rhyme (e.g., please set the kite right).	"try to light the fire"
Cliché	This is a saying or expression that is overused to the point that it has lost its original meaning.	"only time will tell" "At the end of the day…"
Diction	This is the distinctive tone and style of an author.	The author might prefer to use formal language instead of informal language such as slang.
Flashback	This unveils to the reader what happened in the past.	A character is getting ready to do something and, in that moment, recalls a memory that is related to the present moment.
Foreshadowing	These are hints or warnings the author gives the reader about the outcome without ruining the suspense.	The following is foreshadowing change: *The same old thinking and the same old results.*
Irony	This is used to depict a sharp contrast between how things unfold and how they were expected to unfold.	"The judge was put in jail." This is ironic because judges usually put people in jail, not the other way around.
Metaphor	A word or phrase is applied to an object or action to which it is not literally applicable.	She was the moon, illuminating the darkness.
Mood	This is often confused with tone; mood is not the author's attitude but how the readers are made to feel as a result.	Readers can feel *amused, energetic, excited, blissful*, etc.
Parable	This teaches a moral or religious lesson.	Well-known examples of parable are "The Good Samaritan" and "The Prodigal Son."

Device	Definition	Example
Paradox	This is juxtaposing contradictory concepts that when put together revel some hidden truth or significant value.	"Your enemy's friend is your enemy."
Personification	Assigning human characteristics to something nonhuman, or the representation of an abstract quality in human form.	The tree stood tall and proud in the woods, having withstood all the storms in life.
Point of view	This is about who tells the story and how that determines the way the story unfolds and influences the tone.	An objective outsider A first-person account A third-person account
Satire	This is when the author is using humor and making fun of a human flaw not to entertain or amuse the reader, but to get the reader to feel contempt for the subject. Satire is beyond sarcasm.	An example would be when political cartoons use humor to attack political issues.
Simile	Comparing something using the words *like* or *as*.	Her personality was like a wet, cold, blanket
Symbolism	A symbol has layers of figurative meaning to give the object a greater meaning than its literal meaning.	The *dove* is a symbol of peace.
Tone	This is the perspective or attitude of the author with an intended effect on the reader.	Author's tone can be *joyful, humorous, pessimistic,* etc.

Test Tip

We get asked these questions a lot, so we wanted to address them all in one place

Question: Should I indent paragraphs or use a space between them?

Answer: It doesn't matter; just be sure you have definitive paragraphs.

Question: For the quoted text, should I italicize use quotation marks?

Answer: It doesn't matter; just be sure the reader can see that you are quoting the text.

Question: Do I need formal citations?

Answer: No. See the sample responses and notice how the responses simply uses quotes to indicate a quotation.

Steps to passing the Constructed Response Section

The following are a few tips on how to manage your time, plan your essay, apply a proven formula, and proof your essay.

Make a plan

Use the scratch paper the test center provides to map your response or write down a few ideas. This will help you stay organized and concise. Do not spend a lot of time on mapping; just write something down that you can follow as you type the essay.

Keep it organized

Organization is KEY when trying to gain points on the constructed response section. Make it easy on the graders by keeping everything within the formula or framework we just described. Reference the steps below on how to write your constructed responses.

Step 1: Establish a definitive answer or answers to the task or question

Step 2: Use your scratch paper to quickly jot down your ideas and support and set up a simple organizational structure.

Step 3: Construct your paragraph(s). Be sure you are using specifics from the passage.

Step 4: Proof. Be sure to take a moment to proof this part of your response before moving onto the task.

Sample Constructed Responses

Question 1

Analysis: Interpreting Literature

Read carefully the following poem, *Daybreak in Alabama* by Langston Hughes. Then using at least two examples from the poem, describe how Hughes uses imagery and sensory details to describe his ideal world.

Daybreak in Alabama

by Langston Hughes

When I get to be a colored composer
I'm gonna write me some music about
Daybreak in Alabama
And I'm gonna put the purtiest songs in it
Rising out of the ground like a swamp mist
And falling out of heaven like soft dew
I'm gonna put some tall tall trees in it
And the scent of pine needles
And the smell of red clay after rain
And long red necks
And poppy colored faces
And big brown arms
And the field daisy eyes
Of black and white black white black people
And I'm gonna put white hands
And black hands and brown and yellow hands
And red clay earth hands in it
Touching everybody with kind fingers
Touching each other natural as dew
In that dawn of music when I
Get to be a colored composer
And write about daybreak
In Alabama.

Test Tip

Remember, you are not going to summarize the poem. Instead, you are going to find specific images and sensory details to explain the meaning of the poem.

Constructed Response Score of 3

Langston Hughes' ideal world is an integrated Alabama where Black is beautiful and Black and White people live and work together. In the poem Daybreak in Alabama, Langston Hughes uses sensory details like, "the scent of pine needles and the smell of red clay after rain," to describe Alabama. He then uses natural images to describe Black people as beautiful, "And long red necks, and poppy colored faces, and big brown arms, and the field daisy eyes." He also integrates people of different races when he uses the images in these lines, "And I'm gonna put white hands, And black hands and brown and yellow hands, And red clay earth hands in it, Touching everybody with kind fingers, Touching each other natural as dew." The term natural as dew is another reference to nature, implying that Black and White people living in an integrated society is natural or biological. While Alabama is often associated with racial segregation, Langston Hughes desegregates the southern state in his poem Daybreak in Alabama.

Test Tip

Notice that nowhere in the poem does Langston Hughes say the word *desegregation,* yet the reader derives this meaning from the poem by using a critical approach. That is the difference between a score of 1 and a score of 3. Simply summarizing the poem is not enough. Instead, find implicit meaning and explain it in your essay by using a critical approach.

Let's check this constructed response against the rubric score of 3.

Required for a score of 3	Evidence from the response
☑ Analyzes the specified elements in the selection accurately with some depth.	The response references the specific images the author uses in the poem and explains how they contribute to the author's ideal world.
☑ Shows sound understanding of the selection.	The response demonstrates an understanding of the meaning of the poem in general as well as specific details of the poem.
☑ Supports points with appropriate examples from the selection and explains how the examples support the points.	Specific details are referenced. The task calls for at least 2, and the response references more than that. The response also describes specific details regarding how they are used and the effect they have on the poem's meaning.
☑ Is coherent and demonstrates control of language, including diction and syntax.	The response is cohesive, organized, and demonstrates proper diction and syntax.
☑ Demonstrates facility with the conventions of standard written English.	The grammar and conventions are sound with little to no errors.

Question 2

Analysis: Evaluating Rhetorical Features

Read carefully the following excerpt from the book *How to Read Literature Like a Professor* by Thomas C. Foster. Then identify the tone of the passage and describe how Foster develops the tone of the passage. Use specific examples from the excerpt in your response.

If It's a Square, It's a Sonnet

Every few class periods, I'll begin discussion by asking the class what form the poem under consideration employs. That first time, the correct answer will be "sonnet." The next time it happens, "sonnet." Care to guess about the third? Very astute. Basically, I figure the sonnet is the only poetic form the great majority of readers ever needs to know. First, most readers will go through life without ever doing any intensive study of poetry, while many poetic forms require in-depth analysis to be recognized. Moreover, there just aren't that many villanelles in the world for us to see them very often.

The sonnet, on the other hand, is blessedly common, has been written in every era since the English Renaissance, and remains very popular with poets and readers today. Best of all, it has a look. Other forms require mnemonic assistance. It doesn't take any great sagacity to know that Ezra Pound's "Sestina: Altaforte" (1909) is actually a sestina, but I for one am very grateful that he labels it as to form. We would notice that something funny is going on, that in fact he uses the same six words to end the lines in every stanza, but who has a name for that? We can learn to put the name "villanelle" to Theodore Roethke's "The Waking" (1953), but most readers don't carry that information around with them. Or need to, really. Is the quality of your life harmed by not recognizing on sight something like the rondeau? That's what I thought. And so, unless your ambitions have been spurred by this discussion, I'll stick to the sonnet, for one single reason: no other poem is so versatile, so ubiquitous, so various, so agreeably short as the sonnet.

Constructed Response Score of 3

The tone of the passage by Thomas Foster is arrogant. The reader gets the sense of Foster's snobbery right from the beginning when he pokes fun at his students for not knowing any other type of poetry other than a sonnet. The line that solidifies his haughtiness is, "First, most readers will go through life without ever doing any intensive study of poetry, while many poetic forms require in-depth analysis to be recognized." This gives off a type of superiority when it comes to analyzing literature. He then talks about how the sonnet is "blessedly common," which he equates to most readers. The word "common" comes off as pretentious and rude because common, in this case, means simple or uneducated. Then he goes on to show how smart he is by describing other poems most people know nothing about "Ezra Pound's 'Sestina: Altaforte' is actually a sestina," and "We can learn to put the name 'villanelle' to Theodore Roethke's 'The Waking.'" Finally, he ends with one last over-confident dig when he says, "I'll stick to the sonnet, for one single reason: no other poem is so versatile, so ubiquitous, so various, so agreeably short as the sonnet." This implies that people prefer short literature or poetry and don't really want to do the literary analysis for any other type of poem. The line "so agreeably short" reinforces his discount for the average reader of literature.

Quick Tip

Notice that there are different words used in the constructed response for the term *arrogant*. The writer uses snobbery, haughtiness, pretentious, superiority. This helps to drive the point that the author is a snob, without using the word snob over and over again.

Let's check this constructed response against the rubric score of 3.

Required for a score of 3	Evidence from the response
☑ Analyzes the specified elements in the selection accurately with some depth.	The response references the specific lines when the author comes off as arrogant.
☑ Shows sound understanding of the selection.	The response demonstrates an understanding of the meaning of the piece and uses support to back up claims made.
☑ Supports points with appropriate examples from the selection and explains how the examples support the points.	Specific details are referenced. The writer makes an observation that Foster is arrogant and then goes onto show several areas in the passage that supports that observation.
☑ Is coherent and demonstrates control of language, including diction and syntax.	The response is cohesive, organized, and demonstrates proper diction and syntax.
☑ Demonstrates facility with the conventions of standard written English.	The grammar and conventions are sound with little to no errors.

Think about it!

Did you find the author's tone to be arrogant? Maybe not. However, that doesn't matter. The sample response says the tone is arrogant and then backs up that claim with specifics. You may have found the tone to be helpful. In that case, find areas that support that claim. There is no "correct" answer when analyzing a piece of text. The most important thing is that you support your claims with evidence from the text.

Question 1

Analysis: Interpreting Literature

Using a critical approach, describe how the author uses the image of water and evaluate the effectiveness/effect on the reader. Support your analysis with textual evidence.

"Not Bad, Dad, Not Bad"
By Jan Heller Levi

I think you are most yourself when you are swimming;
slicing the water with each stroke,
the funny way you breathe, your mouth cocked
as though you're yawning.

You're neither fantastic nor miserable
at getting from here to there.
You wouldn't win any medals, Dad,
but you wouldn't drown.

I think how different everything might have been
had I judged your sidestroke, your butterfly,
your Australian crawl.

But I always thought I was drowning
in that icy ocean between us,
I always thought you were moving too slowly to save me,
When you were moving as fast as you can.

Constructed Response Score of 3

In the poem "Not Bad, Dad, Not Bad" Jan Levi uses images of water to affect the reader. Water, often associated with baptism or forgiveness, is a central theme in the poem. In the first stanza, the father is clumsily swimming in the pool, doing his best to breathe. The author equates this clumsiness to her father's parenting skills. She later relents that she should have judged her father's parenting skills like she judged his swimming. The reference to water is more than just what is in the pool. The water image reinforces the forgiveness the author feels toward her father, further supporting the baptismal theme in the poem.

In the last stanza, water is used differently—as an ominous image of an icy ocean where she would drown because the father is too slow to save her. This image represents the resentment or hurt she felt when she was younger. However, in the last line, forgiveness is presented again when she says, "…I always thought you were moving too slowly to save me, when you were moving as fast as you can." The icy ocean she felt as a child or young adult turns from threatening to baptismal as she exonerates her father for his inability to love her the way she needed him to.

Let's check this constructed response against the rubric score of 3.

	Required for a score of 3	Evidence from the response
☑	Analyzes the specified elements in the selection accurately with some depth.	The response clearly evaluates the image of water as it's used in the poem.
☑	Shows sound understanding of the selection.	The response demonstrates an understanding of the meaning of the piece and uses a critical approach to describe the meaning of the poem.
☑	Supports points with appropriate examples from the selection and explains how the examples support the points.	Specific details are referenced. The writer makes 2 clear observations of how water is used and backs that up with specific lines within the poem to support those claims.
☑	Is coherent and demonstrates control of language, including diction and syntax.	The response is cohesive, organized, and demonstrates proper diction and syntax.
☑	Demonstrates facility with the conventions of standard written English.	The grammar and conventions are sound with little to no errors.

Question 2

Analysis: Evaluating Rhetorical Features

Read the following excerpt from the essay _The Assault on Public Education_ by Noam Chomsky. Then in your own words, identify the main idea of the passage and explain how the method of development and style clarify and support the main idea. Be sure to refer to specific examples from the excerpt in your discussion.

Mass public education is one of the great achievements of American society. It has had many dimensions. One purpose was to prepare independent farmers for life as wage laborers who would tolerate what they regarded as virtual slavery.

The coercive element did not pass without notice. Ralph Waldo Emerson observed that political leaders call for popular education because they fear that "This country is filling up with thousands and millions of voters, and you must educate them to keep them from our throats." But educated the right way: Limit their perspectives and understanding, discourage free and independent thought, and train them for obedience.

"The Masters of Mankind" pursue their "vile maxim"—all for ourselves and nothing for other people," as Adam Smith explained long ago—and its implementation has regularly called forth resistance, which in turn evokes the same fears among the elite. Forty years ago, there was deep concern that the population was breaking free of apathy and obedience.

Since then, many measures have been taken to restore discipline. One is the crusade for privatization – placing control in reliable hands.

Another is sharp increases in tuition, up nearly 600 percent since 1980. These produce a higher education system with "far more economic stratification than is true of any other country," according to Jane Wellman, former director of the Delta Cost Project, which monitors these issues. Tuition increases trap students into long-term debt and hence subordination to private power.

Constructed Response Score of 3

The main idea of the passage is that public education is used not to educate people but to control people. The author, Noam Chomsky, starts and ends with the idea that education is used to trap people into obedience, the opposite of what education is supposed to do, which is liberate people. The piece uses strong, cynical language and examples to support this claim. One example Chomsky uses is that politicians want to keep the masses educated but educated in a certain way so they can control people—"Limit their perspectives and understanding, discourage free and independent thought, and train them for obedience." He uses a quote from Emmerson to support this—"This country is filling up with thousands and millions of voters, and you must educate them to keep them from our throats." Chomsky also references the "vile maximum" by Adam Smith, which pushes for public obedience while only a few benefit and everyone else loses. When the public catches onto this and tries to break free, measures are put in place to keep the masses down, such as privatization and increases in tuition, which further trap students into long-term debt and submission. Finally, he uses a quote from a current researcher, Jane Wellman, to drive home the point that high tuition costs continue to keep students in long-term debt, which is a type of virtual slavery that Chomsky mentions in the beginning of his piece.

Let's check this constructed response against the rubric score of 3.

	Required for a score of 3	Evidence from the response
☑	Analyzes the specified elements in the selection accurately with some depth.	The response clearly evaluates the main idea of the passage and uses examples.
☑	Shows sound understanding of the selection.	The response demonstrates an understanding of the meaning of the piece and uses a critical approach to describe the meaning of the passage—that students are essentially controlled and manipulated by public education, so a small percentage of people benefit while the others lose.
☑	Supports points with appropriate examples from the selection and explains how the examples support the points.	Specific details are referenced including direct quotes to support assertions.
☑	Is coherent and demonstrates control of language, including diction and syntax.	The response is cohesive, organized, and demonstrates proper diction and syntax.
☑	Demonstrates facility with the conventions of standard written English.	The grammar and conventions are sound with little to no errors.

Bibliography

Achieve the Core. (n.d.). Text complexity. Retrieved from https://achievethecore.org/page/2725/text-complexity

Ambridge, B., & Lieven, E. V. M. (2011). *Child language acquisition: Contrasting theoretical approaches.* Cambridge, UK: Cambridge University Press.

"Among" Or "Amongst"? (n.d.). In *Lexico.* Retrieved from https://www.lexico.com/en/grammar/among-or-amongst

Audience Analysis. (2019). Retrieved from https://www.comm.pitt.edu/oral-comm-lab/audience-analysis

Beck, R. B., Black, L., Krieger, L. S., Naylor, P. C., & Shabaka, D. I. (Eds.). (2010). *Modern world history: Patterns of interaction.* Michigan: McDougal Littell.

Bloom, B., Englehart, M. Furst, E., Hill, W., & Krathwohl, D. (1956). *Taxonomy of educational objectives, Handbook I:* The cognitive domain. New York: Longman.

Burley-Allen, M. (1995). *Listening: The forgotten skills: A self-teaching guide* (2nd ed.). New York: Wiley.

Common Core State Standards. (2019). English language arts standards. Retrieved from http://www.corestandards.org/ELA-Literacy/

Dartmouth College. (2015). Conducting writing workshops. Retrieved from https://writing-speech.dartmouth.edu/teaching/first-year-writing-pedagogies-methods-design/conducting-writing-workshops

Dean, D. (2006). *Strategic writing: The writing process and beyond in the secondary English classroom.* Urbana, IL: NCTE.

Dymock, S. (2005). Teaching expository text structure awareness. *The Reading Teacher, 59*(2), 177-181.

Folse, K. (2009). *Keys to teaching grammar to English language learners: A practical handbook.* Ann Arbor: University of Michigan Press.

Gonzalez, J. (2014). 12 ways to support English language learners in the mainstream classroom. Retrieved from https://www.cultofpedagogy.com/supporting-esl-students-mainstream-classroom/

Gunning, T. G. (2002). *Assessing and correcting reading and writing difficulties* (2nd ed.). Boston: Allyn and Bacon.

Haynes, J (2005). Stages of second language acquisition. Retrieved from http://www.everythingesl.net/inservices/language_stages.php

Johnson, M. (2016). Bias in news sources. Retrieved from https://mediasmarts.ca/sites/mediasmarts/files/pdfs/lesson-plan/Lesson_Bias_News_Sources.pdf

Kennedy, X. J. & Gioia, D. (1995). *Literature: An Introduction to Fiction, Poetry, and Drama* (6th ed.). New York: HarperCollins.

Krashen, S.D. & Terrell, T.D. (1983). *The natural approach: Language acquisition in the classroom.* London: Prentice Hall Europe

Kruidenier, J. (2002). Research-based principles for adult basic education: Reading instruction. Portsmouth: NH. RMC Research Corporation.

Lapp, D., Moss, B., Grant, M., and Johnson, K. (2015). Close look at close reading: teaching students to analyze complex texts, grades K–5. Retrieved from http://www.ascd.org/publications/books/114008/chapters/Understanding-and-Evaluating-Text-Complexity.aspx

Larsen-Freeman, D., & Long, M. H. (1991). *An introduction to second language research.* London: Longman.

Linan-Thompson, S., & Vaughn, S. (2007). *Research-based methods of reading instruction for English language learners, grades K-4*. Alexandria, Va.: Association for Supervision and Curriculum Development.

LiteraryDevices Editors. (2013). What are literary devices? Retrieved August 1, 2019, from //literarydevices. net/metaphor/

Lyon, G. R., & Moats, L. C. (1997). Critical conceptual and methodological considerations in reading intervention research. *Journal of Learning Disabilities, 30,* 578-588.

National Council for Teachers of English. (2006). Purpose and audience analysis. Retrieved from http:// www.readwritethink.org/files/resources/lesson_images/lesson948/purpose-audience.pdf

North Hennpin Community College (n.d.). *Basic steps in the research process*. Retrieved from https://www. nhcc.edu/student-resources/library/doinglibraryresearch/basic-steps-in-the-research-process

Sternberg, B. J., Kaplan, K. A., & Borck, J. E. (2007). Enhancing adolescent literacy achievement through integration of technology in the classroom. *Reading Research Quarterly, 42,* 416-420

Suskie, L. (2018). Assessing student learning: A common sense guide (3rd ed.). San Francisco, CA: Wiley.

Warwick, C. (2011). Help…I've been asked to synthesize! Retrieved from https://www.bgsu.edu/content/ dam/BGSU/learning-commons/documents/writing/synthesis/asked-to-synthesize.pdf

Webb, N. (1997). Research monograph no. 6: Criteria for alignment of expectations and Assessments in mathematics and science education. Washington, DC: Council of Chief State School Officers.

Weselby, C. (2014). What is differentiated instruction? Examples of how to differentiate instruction in the classroom. Retrieved from https://education.cu-portland.edu/blog/classroom-resources/examples-of-differentiated-instruction/

WIDA (2012). The English language development standards. Retrieved from https://wida.wisc.edu/sites/ default/files/resource/2012-ELD-Standards.pdf

Made in United States
North Haven, CT
08 February 2024

48476035R00115